DATE:

MY TRADING RULES

DATE:

LOOKED FOR KEY SUPPORT &RESISTANCE LEVELS?	Y	N
ANALYSED YESTERDAY'S SESSION?	Y	N

		CHART ANALYSIS AND REASONS FOR ENTRY
TIME		
QUANTITY		
BUY PRICE		
SELL PRICE		
PROFIT (%)		
RISK REWARD		

WHAT I LEARNT FROM THIS TRADE		
WAS I IN THE CORRECT STATE OF MIND TO ENTER THIS TRADE?	Y	N
DID I USE POSITION SIZING PROPERLY?	Y	N
DID I FOLLOW ALL MY RULES?	Y	N
DID I REPEAT ANY OF MY OLD MISTAKES?	Y	N
AM I A BETTER TRADER THAN YESTERDAY?	Y	N

"The pain you feel today is the strength you feel tomorrow. For every challenge encountered, there is opportunity for growth."

DATE:

LOOKED FOR KEY SUPPORT &RESISTANCE LEVELS?	Y	N
ANALYSED YESTERDAY'S SESSION?	Y	N

		CHART ANALYSIS AND REASONS FOR ENTRY
TIME		
QUANTITY		
BUY PRICE		
SELL PRICE		
PROFIT (%)		
RISK REWARD		

WHAT I LEARNT FROM THIS TRADE		
WAS I IN THE CORRECT STATE OF MIND TO ENTER THIS TRADE?	Y	N
DID I USE POSITION SIZING PROPERLY?	Y	N
DID I FOLLOW ALL MY RULES?	Y	N
DID I REPEAT ANY OF MY OLD MISTAKES?	Y	N
AM I A BETTER TRADER THAN YESTERDAY?	Y	N

"The only way to achieve the impossible is to believe it is possible."

DATE:

LOOKED FOR KEY SUPPORT &RESISTANCE LEVELS?	Y	N
ANALYSED YESTERDAY'S SESSION?	Y	N

TIME	
QUANTITY	
BUY PRICE	
SELL PRICE	
PROFIT (%)	
RISK REWARD	

CHART ANALYSIS AND REASONS FOR ENTRY

WHAT I LEARNT FROM THIS TRADE

WAS I IN THE CORRECT STATE OF MIND TO ENTER THIS TRADE?	Y	N
DID I USE POSITION SIZING PROPERLY?	Y	N
DID I FOLLOW ALL MY RULES?	Y	N
DID I REPEAT ANY OF MY OLD MISTAKES?	Y	N
AM I A BETTER TRADER THAN YESTERDAY?	Y	N

"Positive thinking will let you do everything better than negative thinking will."

DATE:

LOOKED FOR KEY SUPPORT &RESISTANCE LEVELS?	Y	N
ANALYSED YESTERDAY'S SESSION?	Y	N

TIME	
QUANTITY	
BUY PRICE	
SELL PRICE	
PROFIT (%)	
RISK REWARD	

CHART ANALYSIS AND REASONS FOR ENTRY

WHAT I LEARNT FROM THIS TRADE

WAS I IN THE CORRECT STATE OF MIND TO ENTER THIS TRADE?	Y	N
DID I USE POSITION SIZING PROPERLY?	Y	N
DID I FOLLOW ALL MY RULES?	Y	N
DID I REPEAT ANY OF MY OLD MISTAKES?	Y	N
AM I A BETTER TRADER THAN YESTERDAY?	Y	N

"The journey of a thousand miles begins with one step."

DATE:

LOOKED FOR KEY SUPPORT &RESISTANCE LEVELS?	Y	N
ANALYSED YESTERDAY'S SESSION?	Y	N

		CHART ANALYSIS AND REASONS FOR ENTRY
TIME		
QUANTITY		
BUY PRICE		
SELL PRICE		
PROFIT (%)		
RISK REWARD		

WHAT I LEARNT FROM THIS TRADE		
WAS I IN THE CORRECT STATE OF MIND TO ENTER THIS TRADE?	Y	N
DID I USE POSITION SIZING PROPERLY?	Y	N
DID I FOLLOW ALL MY RULES?	Y	N
DID I REPEAT ANY OF MY OLD MISTAKES?	Y	N
AM I A BETTER TRADER THAN YESTERDAY?	Y	N

"Keep your face always toward the sunshine – and shadows will fall behind you."

DATE:

LOOKED FOR KEY SUPPORT &RESISTANCE LEVELS?	Y	N
ANALYSED YESTERDAY'S SESSION?	Y	N

		CHART ANALYSIS AND REASONS FOR ENTRY
TIME		
QUANTITY		
BUY PRICE		
SELL PRICE		
PROFIT (%)		
RISK REWARD		

WHAT I LEARNT FROM THIS TRADE		
WAS I IN THE CORRECT STATE OF MIND TO ENTER THIS TRADE?	Y	N
DID I USE POSITION SIZING PROPERLY?	Y	N
DID I FOLLOW ALL MY RULES?	Y	N
DID I REPEAT ANY OF MY OLD MISTAKES?	Y	N
AM I A BETTER TRADER THAN YESTERDAY?	Y	N

"Every day may not be good, but there's something good in every day."

DATE:

LOOKED FOR KEY SUPPORT &RESISTANCE LEVELS?	Y	N
ANALYSED YESTERDAY'S SESSION?	Y	N

		CHART ANALYSIS AND REASONS FOR ENTRY
TIME		
QUANTITY		
BUY PRICE		
SELL PRICE		
PROFIT (%)		
RISK REWARD		

WHAT I LEARNT FROM THIS TRADE		
WAS I IN THE CORRECT STATE OF MIND TO ENTER THIS TRADE?	Y	N
DID I USE POSITION SIZING PROPERLY?	Y	N
DID I FOLLOW ALL MY RULES?	Y	N
DID I REPEAT ANY OF MY OLD MISTAKES?	Y	N
AM I A BETTER TRADER THAN YESTERDAY?	Y	N

"Once you replace negative thoughts with positive ones, you'll start having positive results."

DATE:

LOOKED FOR KEY SUPPORT &RESISTANCE LEVELS?	Y	N
ANALYSED YESTERDAY'S SESSION?	Y	N

TIME		CHART ANALYSIS AND REASONS FOR ENTRY
QUANTITY		
BUY PRICE		
SELL PRICE		
PROFIT (%)		
RISK REWARD		

WHAT I LEARNT FROM THIS TRADE

WAS I IN THE CORRECT STATE OF MIND TO ENTER THIS TRADE?	Y	N
DID I USE POSITION SIZING PROPERLY?	Y	N
DID I FOLLOW ALL MY RULES?	Y	N
DID I REPEAT ANY OF MY OLD MISTAKES?	Y	N
AM I A BETTER TRADER THAN YESTERDAY?	Y	N

"In the midst of winter, I found there was, within me, an invincible summer."

DATE:

LOOKED FOR KEY SUPPORT &RESISTANCE LEVELS?	Y	N
ANALYSED YESTERDAY'S SESSION?	Y	N

		CHART ANALYSIS AND REASONS FOR ENTRY
TIME		
QUANTITY		
BUY PRICE		
SELL PRICE		
PROFIT (%)		
RISK REWARD		

WHAT I LEARNT FROM THIS TRADE		
WAS I IN THE CORRECT STATE OF MIND TO ENTER THIS TRADE?	Y	N
DID I USE POSITION SIZING PROPERLY?	Y	N
DID I FOLLOW ALL MY RULES?	Y	N
DID I REPEAT ANY OF MY OLD MISTAKES?	Y	N
AM I A BETTER TRADER THAN YESTERDAY?	Y	N

"The only time you fail is when you fall down and stay down."

DATE:

LOOKED FOR KEY SUPPORT &RESISTANCE LEVELS?		Y	N
ANALYSED YESTERDAY'S SESSION?		Y	N

		CHART ANALYSIS AND REASONS FOR ENTRY
TIME		
QUANTITY		
BUY PRICE		
SELL PRICE		
PROFIT (%)		
RISK REWARD		

WHAT I LEARNT FROM THIS TRADE		
WAS I IN THE CORRECT STATE OF MIND TO ENTER THIS TRADE?	Y	N
DID I USE POSITION SIZING PROPERLY?	Y	N
DID I FOLLOW ALL MY RULES?	Y	N
DID I REPEAT ANY OF MY OLD MISTAKES?	Y	N
AM I A BETTER TRADER THAN YESTERDAY?	Y	N

"When you focus on the good, the good gets better."

DATE:

LOOKED FOR KEY SUPPORT &RESISTANCE LEVELS?	Y	N
ANALYSED YESTERDAY'S SESSION?	Y	N

TIME	
QUANTITY	
BUY PRICE	
SELL PRICE	
PROFIT (%)	
RISK REWARD	

CHART ANALYSIS AND REASONS FOR ENTRY

WHAT I LEARNT FROM THIS TRADE

WAS I IN THE CORRECT STATE OF MIND TO ENTER THIS TRADE?	Y	N
DID I USE POSITION SIZING PROPERLY?	Y	N
DID I FOLLOW ALL MY RULES?	Y	N
DID I REPEAT ANY OF MY OLD MISTAKES?	Y	N
AM I A BETTER TRADER THAN YESTERDAY?	Y	N

"Every day may not be good, but there's something good in every day."

DATE:

LOOKED FOR KEY SUPPORT &RESISTANCE LEVELS?	Y	N
ANALYSED YESTERDAY'S SESSION?	Y	N

		CHART ANALYSIS AND REASONS FOR ENTRY
TIME		
QUANTITY		
BUY PRICE		
SELL PRICE		
PROFIT (%)		
RISK REWARD		

WHAT I LEARNT FROM THIS TRADE		
WAS I IN THE CORRECT STATE OF MIND TO ENTER THIS TRADE?	Y	N
DID I USE POSITION SIZING PROPERLY?	Y	N
DID I FOLLOW ALL MY RULES?	Y	N
DID I REPEAT ANY OF MY OLD MISTAKES?	Y	N
AM I A BETTER TRADER THAN YESTERDAY?	Y	N

The greatest glory in living lies not in never falling, but in rising every time we fall.

DATE:

LOOKED FOR KEY SUPPORT &RESISTANCE LEVELS?		Y	N
ANALYSED YESTERDAY'S SESSION?		Y	N

TIME	
QUANTITY	
BUY PRICE	
SELL PRICE	
PROFIT (%)	
RISK REWARD	

CHART ANALYSIS AND REASONS FOR ENTRY

WHAT I LEARNT FROM THIS TRADE

WAS I IN THE CORRECT STATE OF MIND TO ENTER THIS TRADE?	Y	N
DID I USE POSITION SIZING PROPERLY?	Y	N
DID I FOLLOW ALL MY RULES?	Y	N
DID I REPEAT ANY OF MY OLD MISTAKES?	Y	N
AM I A BETTER TRADER THAN YESTERDAY?	Y	N

If you set your goals ridiculously high and it's a failure, you will fail above everyone else's success.

DATE:

LOOKED FOR KEY SUPPORT &RESISTANCE LEVELS?	Y	N
ANALYSED YESTERDAY'S SESSION?	Y	N

		CHART ANALYSIS AND REASONS FOR ENTRY
TIME		
QUANTITY		
BUY PRICE		
SELL PRICE		
PROFIT (%)		
RISK REWARD		

WHAT I LEARNT FROM THIS TRADE		
WAS I IN THE CORRECT STATE OF MIND TO ENTER THIS TRADE?	Y	N
DID I USE POSITION SIZING PROPERLY?	Y	N
DID I FOLLOW ALL MY RULES?	Y	N
DID I REPEAT ANY OF MY OLD MISTAKES?	Y	N
AM I A BETTER TRADER THAN YESTERDAY?	Y	N

It is during our darkest moments that we must focus to see the light.

Be yourself; everyone else is already taken.

DATE:

LOOKED FOR KEY SUPPORT &RESISTANCE LEVELS?	Y	N
ANALYSED YESTERDAY'S SESSION?	Y	N

		CHART ANALYSIS AND REASONS FOR ENTRY
TIME		
QUANTITY		
BUY PRICE		
SELL PRICE		
PROFIT (%)		
RISK REWARD		

WHAT I LEARNT FROM THIS TRADE		

WAS I IN THE CORRECT STATE OF MIND TO ENTER THIS TRADE?	Y	N
DID I USE POSITION SIZING PROPERLY?	Y	N
DID I FOLLOW ALL MY RULES?	Y	N
DID I REPEAT ANY OF MY OLD MISTAKES?	Y	N
AM I A BETTER TRADER THAN YESTERDAY?	Y	N

You will face many defeats in life, but never let yourself be defeated.

DATE:

LOOKED FOR KEY SUPPORT &RESISTANCE LEVELS?	Y	N
ANALYSED YESTERDAY'S SESSION?	Y	N

		CHART ANALYSIS AND REASONS FOR ENTRY
TIME		
QUANTITY		
BUY PRICE		
SELL PRICE		
PROFIT (%)		
RISK REWARD		

WHAT I LEARNT FROM THIS TRADE		
WAS I IN THE CORRECT STATE OF MIND TO ENTER THIS TRADE?	Y	N
DID I USE POSITION SIZING PROPERLY?	Y	N
DID I FOLLOW ALL MY RULES?	Y	N
DID I REPEAT ANY OF MY OLD MISTAKES?	Y	N
AM I A BETTER TRADER THAN YESTERDAY?	Y	N

Go confidently in the direction of your dreams! Live the life you've imagined

DATE:

LOOKED FOR KEY SUPPORT &RESISTANCE LEVELS?	Y	N
ANALYSED YESTERDAY'S SESSION?	Y	N

TIME	
QUANTITY	
BUY PRICE	
SELL PRICE	
PROFIT (%)	
RISK REWARD	

CHART ANALYSIS AND REASONS FOR ENTRY

WHAT I LEARNT FROM THIS TRADE

WAS I IN THE CORRECT STATE OF MIND TO ENTER THIS TRADE?	Y	N
DID I USE POSITION SIZING PROPERLY?	Y	N
DID I FOLLOW ALL MY RULES?	Y	N
DID I REPEAT ANY OF MY OLD MISTAKES?	Y	N
AM I A BETTER TRADER THAN YESTERDAY?	Y	N

Never let the fear of striking out keep you from playing the game.

DATE:

LOOKED FOR KEY SUPPORT &RESISTANCE LEVELS?	Y	N
ANALYSED YESTERDAY'S SESSION?	Y	N

TIME	
QUANTITY	
BUY PRICE	
SELL PRICE	
PROFIT (%)	
RISK REWARD	

CHART ANALYSIS AND REASONS FOR ENTRY

WHAT I LEARNT FROM THIS TRADE

WAS I IN THE CORRECT STATE OF MIND TO ENTER THIS TRADE?	Y	N
DID I USE POSITION SIZING PROPERLY?	Y	N
DID I FOLLOW ALL MY RULES?	Y	N
DID I REPEAT ANY OF MY OLD MISTAKES?	Y	N
AM I A BETTER TRADER THAN YESTERDAY?	Y	N

Many of life's failures are people who did not realize how close they were to success when they gave up.

DATE:

LOOKED FOR KEY SUPPORT &RESISTANCE LEVELS?	Y	N
ANALYSED YESTERDAY'S SESSION?	Y	N

		CHART ANALYSIS AND REASONS FOR ENTRY
TIME		
QUANTITY		
BUY PRICE		
SELL PRICE		
PROFIT (%)		
RISK REWARD		

WHAT I LEARNT FROM THIS TRADE		
WAS I IN THE CORRECT STATE OF MIND TO ENTER THIS TRADE?	Y	N
DID I USE POSITION SIZING PROPERLY?	Y	N
DID I FOLLOW ALL MY RULES?	Y	N
DID I REPEAT ANY OF MY OLD MISTAKES?	Y	N
AM I A BETTER TRADER THAN YESTERDAY?	Y	N

You have brains in your head. You have feet in your shoes. You can steer yourself any direction you choose.

DATE:

LOOKED FOR KEY SUPPORT &RESISTANCE LEVELS?	Y	N
ANALYSED YESTERDAY'S SESSION?	Y	N

		CHART ANALYSIS AND REASONS FOR ENTRY
TIME		
QUANTITY		
BUY PRICE		
SELL PRICE		
PROFIT (%)		
RISK REWARD		

WHAT I LEARNT FROM THIS TRADE		
WAS I IN THE CORRECT STATE OF MIND TO ENTER THIS TRADE?	Y	N
DID I USE POSITION SIZING PROPERLY?	Y	N
DID I FOLLOW ALL MY RULES?	Y	N
DID I REPEAT ANY OF MY OLD MISTAKES?	Y	N
AM I A BETTER TRADER THAN YESTERDAY?	Y	N

"Don't worry when you are not recognized but strive to be worthy of recognition."

DATE:

REVIEW OF LAST 20 TRADES
Most successful strategy-
Worst performing strategy-
Best time for entry-
The Positives-
The Negatives-

DATE:

LOOKED FOR KEY SUPPORT &RESISTANCE LEVELS?	Y	N
ANALYSED YESTERDAY'S SESSION?	Y	N

		CHART ANALYSIS AND REASONS FOR ENTRY
TIME		
QUANTITY		
BUY PRICE		
SELL PRICE		
PROFIT (%)		
RISK REWARD		

WHAT I LEARNT FROM THIS TRADE

WAS I IN THE CORRECT STATE OF MIND TO ENTER THIS TRADE?	Y	N
DID I USE POSITION SIZING PROPERLY?	Y	N
DID I FOLLOW ALL MY RULES?	Y	N
DID I REPEAT ANY OF MY OLD MISTAKES?	Y	N
AM I A BETTER TRADER THAN YESTERDAY?	Y	N

Life is either a daring adventure or nothing.

DATE:

LOOKED FOR KEY SUPPORT &RESISTANCE LEVELS?		Y	N
ANALYSED YESTERDAY'S SESSION?		Y	N

		CHART ANALYSIS AND REASONS FOR ENTRY
TIME		
QUANTITY		
BUY PRICE		
SELL PRICE		
PROFIT (%)		
RISK REWARD		

WHAT I LEARNT FROM THIS TRADE		
WAS I IN THE CORRECT STATE OF MIND TO ENTER THIS TRADE?	Y	N
DID I USE POSITION SIZING PROPERLY?	Y	N
DID I FOLLOW ALL MY RULES?	Y	N
DID I REPEAT ANY OF MY OLD MISTAKES?	Y	N
AM I A BETTER TRADER THAN YESTERDAY?	Y	N

Success is not final; failure is not fatal: It is the courage to continue that counts

DATE:

LOOKED FOR KEY SUPPORT &RESISTANCE LEVELS?	Y	N
ANALYSED YESTERDAY'S SESSION?	Y	N

		CHART ANALYSIS AND REASONS FOR ENTRY
TIME		
QUANTITY		
BUY PRICE		
SELL PRICE		
PROFIT (%)		
RISK REWARD		

WHAT I LEARNT FROM THIS TRADE		
WAS I IN THE CORRECT STATE OF MIND TO ENTER THIS TRADE?	Y	N
DID I USE POSITION SIZING PROPERLY?	Y	N
DID I FOLLOW ALL MY RULES?	Y	N
DID I REPEAT ANY OF MY OLD MISTAKES?	Y	N
AM I A BETTER TRADER THAN YESTERDAY?	Y	N

Success usually comes to those who are too busy to be looking for it

DATE:

		Y	N
LOOKED FOR KEY SUPPORT &RESISTANCE LEVELS?		Y	N
ANALYSED YESTERDAY'S SESSION?		Y	N

		CHART ANALYSIS AND REASONS FOR ENTRY
TIME		
QUANTITY		
BUY PRICE		
SELL PRICE		
PROFIT (%)		
RISK REWARD		

WHAT I LEARNT FROM THIS TRADE

	Y	N
WAS I IN THE CORRECT STATE OF MIND TO ENTER THIS TRADE?	Y	N
DID I USE POSITION SIZING PROPERLY?	Y	N
DID I FOLLOW ALL MY RULES?	Y	N
DID I REPEAT ANY OF MY OLD MISTAKES?	Y	N
AM I A BETTER TRADER THAN YESTERDAY?	Y	N

If you really look closely, most overnight successes took a long time.

DATE:

LOOKED FOR KEY SUPPORT &RESISTANCE LEVELS?	Y	N
ANALYSED YESTERDAY'S SESSION?	Y	N

		CHART ANALYSIS AND REASONS FOR ENTRY
TIME		
QUANTITY		
BUY PRICE		
SELL PRICE		
PROFIT (%)		
RISK REWARD		

WHAT I LEARNT FROM THIS TRADE		
WAS I IN THE CORRECT STATE OF MIND TO ENTER THIS TRADE?	Y	N
DID I USE POSITION SIZING PROPERLY?	Y	N
DID I FOLLOW ALL MY RULES?	Y	N
DID I REPEAT ANY OF MY OLD MISTAKES?	Y	N
AM I A BETTER TRADER THAN YESTERDAY?	Y	N

The secret of success is to do the common thing uncommonly well.

DATE:

LOOKED FOR KEY SUPPORT &RESISTANCE LEVELS?	Y	N
ANALYSED YESTERDAY'S SESSION?	Y	N

TIME	
QUANTITY	
BUY PRICE	
SELL PRICE	
PROFIT (%)	
RISK REWARD	

CHART ANALYSIS AND REASONS FOR ENTRY

WHAT I LEARNT FROM THIS TRADE

WAS I IN THE CORRECT STATE OF MIND TO ENTER THIS TRADE?	Y	N
DID I USE POSITION SIZING PROPERLY?	Y	N
DID I FOLLOW ALL MY RULES?	Y	N
DID I REPEAT ANY OF MY OLD MISTAKES?	Y	N
AM I A BETTER TRADER THAN YESTERDAY?	Y	N

"Everything you can imagine is real."

DATE:

LOOKED FOR KEY SUPPORT &RESISTANCE LEVELS?	Y	N
ANALYSED YESTERDAY'S SESSION?	Y	N

		CHART ANALYSIS AND REASONS FOR ENTRY
TIME		
QUANTITY		
BUY PRICE		
SELL PRICE		
PROFIT (%)		
RISK REWARD		

WHAT I LEARNT FROM THIS TRADE		

WAS I IN THE CORRECT STATE OF MIND TO ENTER THIS TRADE?	Y	N
DID I USE POSITION SIZING PROPERLY?	Y	N
DID I FOLLOW ALL MY RULES?	Y	N
DID I REPEAT ANY OF MY OLD MISTAKES?	Y	N
AM I A BETTER TRADER THAN YESTERDAY?	Y	N

"Always remember, your focus determines your reality."

DATE:

LOOKED FOR KEY SUPPORT &RESISTANCE LEVELS?	Y	N
ANALYSED YESTERDAY'S SESSION?	Y	N

		CHART ANALYSIS AND REASONS FOR ENTRY
TIME		
QUANTITY		
BUY PRICE		
SELL PRICE		
PROFIT (%)		
RISK REWARD		

WHAT I LEARNT FROM THIS TRADE		

WAS I IN THE CORRECT STATE OF MIND TO ENTER THIS TRADE?	Y	N
DID I USE POSITION SIZING PROPERLY?	Y	N
DID I FOLLOW ALL MY RULES?	Y	N
DID I REPEAT ANY OF MY OLD MISTAKES?	Y	N
AM I A BETTER TRADER THAN YESTERDAY?	Y	N

"Success is walking from failure to failure with no loss of enthusiasm."

DATE:

LOOKED FOR KEY SUPPORT &RESISTANCE LEVELS?	Y	N
ANALYSED YESTERDAY'S SESSION?	Y	N

		CHART ANALYSIS AND REASONS FOR ENTRY
TIME		
QUANTITY		
BUY PRICE		
SELL PRICE		
PROFIT (%)		
RISK REWARD		

WHAT I LEARNT FROM THIS TRADE		

WAS I IN THE CORRECT STATE OF MIND TO ENTER THIS TRADE?	Y	N
DID I USE POSITION SIZING PROPERLY?	Y	N
DID I FOLLOW ALL MY RULES?	Y	N
DID I REPEAT ANY OF MY OLD MISTAKES?	Y	N
AM I A BETTER TRADER THAN YESTERDAY?	Y	N

"When you undervalue what you do, the world will undervalue who you are."

DATE:

LOOKED FOR KEY SUPPORT &RESISTANCE LEVELS?	Y	N
ANALYSED YESTERDAY'S SESSION?	Y	N

		CHART ANALYSIS AND REASONS FOR ENTRY
TIME		
QUANTITY		
BUY PRICE		
SELL PRICE		
PROFIT (%)		
RISK REWARD		

WHAT I LEARNT FROM THIS TRADE		
WAS I IN THE CORRECT STATE OF MIND TO ENTER THIS TRADE?	Y	N
DID I USE POSITION SIZING PROPERLY?	Y	N
DID I FOLLOW ALL MY RULES?	Y	N
DID I REPEAT ANY OF MY OLD MISTAKES?	Y	N
AM I A BETTER TRADER THAN YESTERDAY?	Y	N

"If you want to achieve excellence, you can get there today. As of this second, quit doing less-than-excellent work."

DATE:

LOOKED FOR KEY SUPPORT &RESISTANCE LEVELS?	Y	N
ANALYSED YESTERDAY'S SESSION?	Y	N

		CHART ANALYSIS AND REASONS FOR ENTRY
TIME		
QUANTITY		
BUY PRICE		
SELL PRICE		
PROFIT (%)		
RISK REWARD		

WHAT I LEARNT FROM THIS TRADE		

WAS I IN THE CORRECT STATE OF MIND TO ENTER THIS TRADE?	Y	N
DID I USE POSITION SIZING PROPERLY?	Y	N
DID I FOLLOW ALL MY RULES?	Y	N
DID I REPEAT ANY OF MY OLD MISTAKES?	Y	N
AM I A BETTER TRADER THAN YESTERDAY?	Y	N

"The question isn't who is going to let me; it's who is going to stop me."

DATE:

LOOKED FOR KEY SUPPORT &RESISTANCE LEVELS?	Y	N
ANALYSED YESTERDAY'S SESSION?	Y	N

		CHART ANALYSIS AND REASONS FOR ENTRY
TIME		
QUANTITY		
BUY PRICE		
SELL PRICE		
PROFIT (%)		
RISK REWARD		

WHAT I LEARNT FROM THIS TRADE

WAS I IN THE CORRECT STATE OF MIND TO ENTER THIS TRADE?	Y	N
DID I USE POSITION SIZING PROPERLY?	Y	N
DID I FOLLOW ALL MY RULES?	Y	N
DID I REPEAT ANY OF MY OLD MISTAKES?	Y	N
AM I A BETTER TRADER THAN YESTERDAY?	Y	N

"Everything you've ever wanted is on the other side of fear."

DATE:

LOOKED FOR KEY SUPPORT &RESISTANCE LEVELS?	Y	N
ANALYSED YESTERDAY'S SESSION?	Y	N

TIME	
QUANTITY	
BUY PRICE	
SELL PRICE	
PROFIT (%)	
RISK REWARD	

CHART ANALYSIS AND REASONS FOR ENTRY

WHAT I LEARNT FROM THIS TRADE

WAS I IN THE CORRECT STATE OF MIND TO ENTER THIS TRADE?	Y	N
DID I USE POSITION SIZING PROPERLY?	Y	N
DID I FOLLOW ALL MY RULES?	Y	N
DID I REPEAT ANY OF MY OLD MISTAKES?	Y	N
AM I A BETTER TRADER THAN YESTERDAY?	Y	N

"Nothing is impossible, the word itself says, 'I'm possible!'"

DATE:

LOOKED FOR KEY SUPPORT &RESISTANCE LEVELS?	Y	N
ANALYSED YESTERDAY'S SESSION?	Y	N

		CHART ANALYSIS AND REASONS FOR ENTRY
TIME		
QUANTITY		
BUY PRICE		
SELL PRICE		
PROFIT (%)		
RISK REWARD		

WHAT I LEARNT FROM THIS TRADE		
WAS I IN THE CORRECT STATE OF MIND TO ENTER THIS TRADE?	Y	N
DID I USE POSITION SIZING PROPERLY?	Y	N
DID I FOLLOW ALL MY RULES?	Y	N
DID I REPEAT ANY OF MY OLD MISTAKES?	Y	N
AM I A BETTER TRADER THAN YESTERDAY?	Y	N

"Lack of direction, not lack of time, is the problem. We all have twenty-four-hour days."

DATE:

LOOKED FOR KEY SUPPORT &RESISTANCE LEVELS?	Y	N
ANALYSED YESTERDAY'S SESSION?	Y	N

TIME	
QUANTITY	
BUY PRICE	
SELL PRICE	
PROFIT (%)	
RISK REWARD	

CHART ANALYSIS AND REASONS FOR ENTRY

WHAT I LEARNT FROM THIS TRADE

WAS I IN THE CORRECT STATE OF MIND TO ENTER THIS TRADE?	Y	N
DID I USE POSITION SIZING PROPERLY?	Y	N
DID I FOLLOW ALL MY RULES?	Y	N
DID I REPEAT ANY OF MY OLD MISTAKES?	Y	N
AM I A BETTER TRADER THAN YESTERDAY?	Y	N

'Play to your strengths. If you aren't great at something, do more of what you're great at.'

DATE:

LOOKED FOR KEY SUPPORT &RESISTANCE LEVELS?	Y	N
ANALYSED YESTERDAY'S SESSION?	Y	N

		CHART ANALYSIS AND REASONS FOR ENTRY
TIME		
QUANTITY		
BUY PRICE		
SELL PRICE		
PROFIT (%)		
RISK REWARD		

WHAT I LEARNT FROM THIS TRADE		
WAS I IN THE CORRECT STATE OF MIND TO ENTER THIS TRADE?	Y	N
DID I USE POSITION SIZING PROPERLY?	Y	N
DID I FOLLOW ALL MY RULES?	Y	N
DID I REPEAT ANY OF MY OLD MISTAKES?	Y	N
AM I A BETTER TRADER THAN YESTERDAY?	Y	N

"I can't change the direction of the wind, but I can adjust my sails to always reach my destination."

DATE:

LOOKED FOR KEY SUPPORT &RESISTANCE LEVELS?	Y	N
ANALYSED YESTERDAY'S SESSION?	Y	N

		CHART ANALYSIS AND REASONS FOR ENTRY
TIME		
QUANTITY		
BUY PRICE		
SELL PRICE		
PROFIT (%)		
RISK REWARD		

WHAT I LEARNT FROM THIS TRADE		
WAS I IN THE CORRECT STATE OF MIND TO ENTER THIS TRADE?	Y	N
DID I USE POSITION SIZING PROPERLY?	Y	N
DID I FOLLOW ALL MY RULES?	Y	N
DID I REPEAT ANY OF MY OLD MISTAKES?	Y	N
AM I A BETTER TRADER THAN YESTERDAY?	Y	N

"The pain you feel today is the strength you feel tomorrow. For every challenge encountered, there is opportunity for growth."

DATE:

LOOKED FOR KEY SUPPORT &RESISTANCE LEVELS?	Y	N
ANALYSED YESTERDAY'S SESSION?	Y	N

		CHART ANALYSIS AND REASONS FOR ENTRY
TIME		
QUANTITY		
BUY PRICE		
SELL PRICE		
PROFIT (%)		
RISK REWARD		

WHAT I LEARNT FROM THIS TRADE		
WAS I IN THE CORRECT STATE OF MIND TO ENTER THIS TRADE?	Y	N
DID I USE POSITION SIZING PROPERLY?	Y	N
DID I FOLLOW ALL MY RULES?	Y	N
DID I REPEAT ANY OF MY OLD MISTAKES?	Y	N
AM I A BETTER TRADER THAN YESTERDAY?	Y	N

"Since we cannot change reality, let us change the eyes which see reality."

DATE:

LOOKED FOR KEY SUPPORT &RESISTANCE LEVELS?	Y	N
ANALYSED YESTERDAY'S SESSION?	Y	N

		CHART ANALYSIS AND REASONS FOR ENTRY
TIME		
QUANTITY		
BUY PRICE		
SELL PRICE		
PROFIT (%)		
RISK REWARD		

WHAT I LEARNT FROM THIS TRADE		
WAS I IN THE CORRECT STATE OF MIND TO ENTER THIS TRADE?	Y	N
DID I USE POSITION SIZING PROPERLY?	Y	N
DID I FOLLOW ALL MY RULES?	Y	N
DID I REPEAT ANY OF MY OLD MISTAKES?	Y	N
AM I A BETTER TRADER THAN YESTERDAY?	Y	N

"Hard work beats talent when talent doesn't work hard."

DATE:

LOOKED FOR KEY SUPPORT &RESISTANCE LEVELS?	Y	N
ANALYSED YESTERDAY'S SESSION?	Y	N

		CHART ANALYSIS AND REASONS FOR ENTRY
TIME		
QUANTITY		
BUY PRICE		
SELL PRICE		
PROFIT (%)		
RISK REWARD		

WHAT I LEARNT FROM THIS TRADE		
WAS I IN THE CORRECT STATE OF MIND TO ENTER THIS TRADE?	Y	N
DID I USE POSITION SIZING PROPERLY?	Y	N
DID I FOLLOW ALL MY RULES?	Y	N
DID I REPEAT ANY OF MY OLD MISTAKES?	Y	N
AM I A BETTER TRADER THAN YESTERDAY?	Y	N

"The only thing standing between you and outrageous success is continuous progress."

DATE:

REVIEW OF LAST 20 TRADES
Most successful strategy-
Worst performing strategy-
Best time for entry-
The Positives-
The Negatives-

DATE:

LOOKED FOR KEY SUPPORT &RESISTANCE LEVELS?	Y	N
ANALYSED YESTERDAY'S SESSION?	Y	N

		CHART ANALYSIS AND REASONS FOR ENTRY
TIME		
QUANTITY		
BUY PRICE		
SELL PRICE		
PROFIT (%)		
RISK REWARD		

WHAT I LEARNT FROM THIS TRADE		
WAS I IN THE CORRECT STATE OF MIND TO ENTER THIS TRADE?	Y	N
DID I USE POSITION SIZING PROPERLY?	Y	N
DID I FOLLOW ALL MY RULES?	Y	N
DID I REPEAT ANY OF MY OLD MISTAKES?	Y	N
AM I A BETTER TRADER THAN YESTERDAY?	Y	N

"Impossible is just an opinion."

LOOKED FOR KEY SUPPORT &RESISTANCE LEVELS?	Y	N

DATE:

ANALYSED YESTERDAY'S SESSION?	Y	N

TIME		CHART ANALYSIS AND REASONS FOR ENTRY
QUANTITY		
BUY PRICE		
SELL PRICE		
PROFIT (%)		
RISK REWARD		

WHAT I LEARNT FROM THIS TRADE		
WAS I IN THE CORRECT STATE OF MIND TO ENTER THIS TRADE?	Y	N
DID I USE POSITION SIZING PROPERLY?	Y	N
DID I FOLLOW ALL MY RULES?	Y	N
DID I REPEAT ANY OF MY OLD MISTAKES?	Y	N
AM I A BETTER TRADER THAN YESTERDAY?	Y	N

"There are no traffic jams on the extra mile."

DATE:

LOOKED FOR KEY SUPPORT &RESISTANCE LEVELS?	Y	N
ANALYSED YESTERDAY'S SESSION?	Y	N

		CHART ANALYSIS AND REASONS FOR ENTRY
TIME		
QUANTITY		
BUY PRICE		
SELL PRICE		
PROFIT (%)		
RISK REWARD		

WHAT I LEARNT FROM THIS TRADE		
WAS I IN THE CORRECT STATE OF MIND TO ENTER THIS TRADE?	Y	N
DID I USE POSITION SIZING PROPERLY?	Y	N
DID I FOLLOW ALL MY RULES?	Y	N
DID I REPEAT ANY OF MY OLD MISTAKES?	Y	N
AM I A BETTER TRADER THAN YESTERDAY?	Y	N

"The greater the difficulty, the more the glory in surmounting it."

DATE:

LOOKED FOR KEY SUPPORT &RESISTANCE LEVELS?	Y	N
ANALYSED YESTERDAY'S SESSION?	Y	N

TIME	
QUANTITY	
BUY PRICE	
SELL PRICE	
PROFIT (%)	
RISK REWARD	

CHART ANALYSIS AND REASONS FOR ENTRY

WHAT I LEARNT FROM THIS TRADE

WAS I IN THE CORRECT STATE OF MIND TO ENTER THIS TRADE?	Y	N
DID I USE POSITION SIZING PROPERLY?	Y	N
DID I FOLLOW ALL MY RULES?	Y	N
DID I REPEAT ANY OF MY OLD MISTAKES?	Y	N
AM I A BETTER TRADER THAN YESTERDAY?	Y	N

"*You are your greatest asset. Put your time, effort, and money into training.*"

DATE:

LOOKED FOR KEY SUPPORT &RESISTANCE LEVELS?	Y	N
ANALYSED YESTERDAY'S SESSION?	Y	N

		CHART ANALYSIS AND REASONS FOR ENTRY
TIME		
QUANTITY		
BUY PRICE		
SELL PRICE		
PROFIT (%)		
RISK REWARD		

WHAT I LEARNT FROM THIS TRADE		
WAS I IN THE CORRECT STATE OF MIND TO ENTER THIS TRADE?	Y	N
DID I USE POSITION SIZING PROPERLY?	Y	N
DID I FOLLOW ALL MY RULES?	Y	N
DID I REPEAT ANY OF MY OLD MISTAKES?	Y	N
AM I A BETTER TRADER THAN YESTERDAY?	Y	N

"There will be obstacles. There will be doubters. There will be mistakes. But with hard work, there are no limits."

DATE:

LOOKED FOR KEY SUPPORT &RESISTANCE LEVELS?	Y	N
ANALYSED YESTERDAY'S SESSION?	Y	N

		CHART ANALYSIS AND REASONS FOR ENTRY
TIME		
QUANTITY		
BUY PRICE		
SELL PRICE		
PROFIT (%)		
RISK REWARD		

WHAT I LEARNT FROM THIS TRADE		
WAS I IN THE CORRECT STATE OF MIND TO ENTER THIS TRADE?	Y	N
DID I USE POSITION SIZING PROPERLY?	Y	N
DID I FOLLOW ALL MY RULES?	Y	N
DID I REPEAT ANY OF MY OLD MISTAKES?	Y	N
AM I A BETTER TRADER THAN YESTERDAY?	Y	N

"Doing the best at this moment puts you in the best place for the next moment."

DATE:

LOOKED FOR KEY SUPPORT &RESISTANCE LEVELS?	Y	N
ANALYSED YESTERDAY'S SESSION?	Y	N

TIME	
QUANTITY	
BUY PRICE	
SELL PRICE	
PROFIT (%)	
RISK REWARD	

CHART ANALYSIS AND REASONS FOR ENTRY

WHAT I LEARNT FROM THIS TRADE

WAS I IN THE CORRECT STATE OF MIND TO ENTER THIS TRADE?	Y	N
DID I USE POSITION SIZING PROPERLY?	Y	N
DID I FOLLOW ALL MY RULES?	Y	N
DID I REPEAT ANY OF MY OLD MISTAKES?	Y	N
AM I A BETTER TRADER THAN YESTERDAY?	Y	N

"Obstacles can't stop you. Problems can't stop you. Most of all, other people can't stop you. Only you can stop you."

DATE:

LOOKED FOR KEY SUPPORT &RESISTANCE LEVELS?	Y	N
ANALYSED YESTERDAY'S SESSION?	Y	N

		CHART ANALYSIS AND REASONS FOR ENTRY
TIME		
QUANTITY		
BUY PRICE		
SELL PRICE		
PROFIT (%)		
RISK REWARD		

WHAT I LEARNT FROM THIS TRADE

WAS I IN THE CORRECT STATE OF MIND TO ENTER THIS TRADE?	Y	N
DID I USE POSITION SIZING PROPERLY?	Y	N
DID I FOLLOW ALL MY RULES?	Y	N
DID I REPEAT ANY OF MY OLD MISTAKES?	Y	N
AM I A BETTER TRADER THAN YESTERDAY?	Y	N

"Our greatest weakness lies in giving up. The most certain way to succeed is always to try just one more time."

DATE:

LOOKED FOR KEY SUPPORT &RESISTANCE LEVELS?	Y	N
ANALYSED YESTERDAY'S SESSION?	Y	N

		CHART ANALYSIS AND REASONS FOR ENTRY
TIME		
QUANTITY		
BUY PRICE		
SELL PRICE		
PROFIT (%)		
RISK REWARD		

WHAT I LEARNT FROM THIS TRADE		

WAS I IN THE CORRECT STATE OF MIND TO ENTER THIS TRADE?	Y	N
DID I USE POSITION SIZING PROPERLY?	Y	N
DID I FOLLOW ALL MY RULES?	Y	N
DID I REPEAT ANY OF MY OLD MISTAKES?	Y	N
AM I A BETTER TRADER THAN YESTERDAY?	Y	N

"Never be limited by other people's limited imaginations."

DATE:

		Y	N
LOOKED FOR KEY SUPPORT &RESISTANCE LEVELS?		Y	N
ANALYSED YESTERDAY'S SESSION?		Y	N

		CHART ANALYSIS AND REASONS FOR ENTRY
TIME		
QUANTITY		
BUY PRICE		
SELL PRICE		
PROFIT (%)		
RISK REWARD		

WHAT I LEARNT FROM THIS TRADE		
WAS I IN THE CORRECT STATE OF MIND TO ENTER THIS TRADE?	Y	N
DID I USE POSITION SIZING PROPERLY?	Y	N
DID I FOLLOW ALL MY RULES?	Y	N
DID I REPEAT ANY OF MY OLD MISTAKES?	Y	N
AM I A BETTER TRADER THAN YESTERDAY?	Y	N

"Success isn't always about greatness. It's about consistency. Consistent hard work leads to success. Greatness will come."

DATE:

LOOKED FOR KEY SUPPORT &RESISTANCE LEVELS?	Y	N
ANALYSED YESTERDAY'S SESSION?	Y	N

		CHART ANALYSIS AND REASONS FOR ENTRY
TIME		
QUANTITY		
BUY PRICE		
SELL PRICE		
PROFIT (%)		
RISK REWARD		

WHAT I LEARNT FROM THIS TRADE		
WAS I IN THE CORRECT STATE OF MIND TO ENTER THIS TRADE?	Y	N
DID I USE POSITION SIZING PROPERLY?	Y	N
DID I FOLLOW ALL MY RULES?	Y	N
DID I REPEAT ANY OF MY OLD MISTAKES?	Y	N
AM I A BETTER TRADER THAN YESTERDAY?	Y	N

"Success is not final; failure is not fatal: It is the courage to continue that counts."

DATE:

LOOKED FOR KEY SUPPORT &RESISTANCE LEVELS?	Y	N
ANALYSED YESTERDAY'S SESSION?	Y	N

		CHART ANALYSIS AND REASONS FOR ENTRY
TIME		
QUANTITY		
BUY PRICE		
SELL PRICE		
PROFIT (%)		
RISK REWARD		

WHAT I LEARNT FROM THIS TRADE		
WAS I IN THE CORRECT STATE OF MIND TO ENTER THIS TRADE?	Y	N
DID I USE POSITION SIZING PROPERLY?	Y	N
DID I FOLLOW ALL MY RULES?	Y	N
DID I REPEAT ANY OF MY OLD MISTAKES?	Y	N
AM I A BETTER TRADER THAN YESTERDAY?	Y	N

"Develop success from failures. Discouragement and failure are two of the surest stepping stones to success.

DATE:

LOOKED FOR KEY SUPPORT &RESISTANCE LEVELS?	Y	N
ANALYSED YESTERDAY'S SESSION?	Y	N

		CHART ANALYSIS AND REASONS FOR ENTRY
TIME		
QUANTITY		
BUY PRICE		
SELL PRICE		
PROFIT (%)		
RISK REWARD		

WHAT I LEARNT FROM THIS TRADE		
WAS I IN THE CORRECT STATE OF MIND TO ENTER THIS TRADE?	Y	N
DID I USE POSITION SIZING PROPERLY?	Y	N
DID I FOLLOW ALL MY RULES?	Y	N
DID I REPEAT ANY OF MY OLD MISTAKES?	Y	N
AM I A BETTER TRADER THAN YESTERDAY?	Y	N

"He who would learn to fly one day must first learn to stand and walk and run and climb and dance; one cannot fly into flying."

DATE:

LOOKED FOR KEY SUPPORT &RESISTANCE LEVELS?	Y	N
ANALYSED YESTERDAY'S SESSION?	Y	N

		CHART ANALYSIS AND REASONS FOR ENTRY
TIME		
QUANTITY		
BUY PRICE		
SELL PRICE		
PROFIT (%)		
RISK REWARD		

WHAT I LEARNT FROM THIS TRADE		
WAS I IN THE CORRECT STATE OF MIND TO ENTER THIS TRADE?	Y	N
DID I USE POSITION SIZING PROPERLY?	Y	N
DID I FOLLOW ALL MY RULES?	Y	N
DID I REPEAT ANY OF MY OLD MISTAKES?	Y	N
AM I A BETTER TRADER THAN YESTERDAY?	Y	N

"A bend in the road is not the end of the road, unless you fail to make the turn."

DATE:

LOOKED FOR KEY SUPPORT &RESISTANCE LEVELS?	Y	N
ANALYSED YESTERDAY'S SESSION?	Y	N

		CHART ANALYSIS AND REASONS FOR ENTRY
TIME		
QUANTITY		
BUY PRICE		
SELL PRICE		
PROFIT (%)		
RISK REWARD		

WHAT I LEARNT FROM THIS TRADE

WAS I IN THE CORRECT STATE OF MIND TO ENTER THIS TRADE?	Y	N
DID I USE POSITION SIZING PROPERLY?	Y	N
DID I FOLLOW ALL MY RULES?	Y	N
DID I REPEAT ANY OF MY OLD MISTAKES?	Y	N
AM I A BETTER TRADER THAN YESTERDAY?	Y	N

"Success is the sum of small efforts, repeated day in and day out."

DATE:

LOOKED FOR KEY SUPPORT &RESISTANCE LEVELS?	Y	N
ANALYSED YESTERDAY'S SESSION?	Y	N

		CHART ANALYSIS AND REASONS FOR ENTRY
TIME		
QUANTITY		
BUY PRICE		
SELL PRICE		
PROFIT (%)		
RISK REWARD		

WHAT I LEARNT FROM THIS TRADE		
WAS I IN THE CORRECT STATE OF MIND TO ENTER THIS TRADE?	Y	N
DID I USE POSITION SIZING PROPERLY?	Y	N
DID I FOLLOW ALL MY RULES?	Y	N
DID I REPEAT ANY OF MY OLD MISTAKES?	Y	N
AM I A BETTER TRADER THAN YESTERDAY?	Y	N

"Don't judge each day by the harvest you reap but by the seeds that you plant."

DATE:

LOOKED FOR KEY SUPPORT &RESISTANCE LEVELS?	Y	N
ANALYSED YESTERDAY'S SESSION?	Y	N

		CHART ANALYSIS AND REASONS FOR ENTRY
TIME		
QUANTITY		
BUY PRICE		
SELL PRICE		
PROFIT (%)		
RISK REWARD		

WHAT I LEARNT FROM THIS TRADE		

WAS I IN THE CORRECT STATE OF MIND TO ENTER THIS TRADE?	Y	N
DID I USE POSITION SIZING PROPERLY?	Y	N
DID I FOLLOW ALL MY RULES?	Y	N
DID I REPEAT ANY OF MY OLD MISTAKES?	Y	N
AM I A BETTER TRADER THAN YESTERDAY?	Y	N

"A diamond is a piece of coal that stuck to the job."

DATE:

LOOKED FOR KEY SUPPORT &RESISTANCE LEVELS?	Y	N
ANALYSED YESTERDAY'S SESSION?	Y	N

		CHART ANALYSIS AND REASONS FOR ENTRY
TIME		
QUANTITY		
BUY PRICE		
SELL PRICE		
PROFIT (%)		
RISK REWARD		

WHAT I LEARNT FROM THIS TRADE		
WAS I IN THE CORRECT STATE OF MIND TO ENTER THIS TRADE?	Y	N
DID I USE POSITION SIZING PROPERLY?	Y	N
DID I FOLLOW ALL MY RULES?	Y	N
DID I REPEAT ANY OF MY OLD MISTAKES?	Y	N
AM I A BETTER TRADER THAN YESTERDAY?	Y	N

"Chop your own wood, and it will warm you twice."

DATE:

			Y	N
LOOKED FOR KEY SUPPORT &RESISTANCE LEVELS?			Y	N
ANALYSED YESTERDAY'S SESSION?			Y	N

		CHART ANALYSIS AND REASONS FOR ENTRY
TIME		
QUANTITY		
BUY PRICE		
SELL PRICE		
PROFIT (%)		
RISK REWARD		

WHAT I LEARNT FROM THIS TRADE		

	Y	N
WAS I IN THE CORRECT STATE OF MIND TO ENTER THIS TRADE?	Y	N
DID I USE POSITION SIZING PROPERLY?	Y	N
DID I FOLLOW ALL MY RULES?	Y	N
DID I REPEAT ANY OF MY OLD MISTAKES?	Y	N
AM I A BETTER TRADER THAN YESTERDAY?	Y	N

Success usually comes to those who are too busy to be looking for it.

DATE:

ANALYSED YESTERDAY'S SESSION?	Y	N
ANALYSED YESTERDAY'S SESSION?	Y	N

		CHART ANALYSIS AND REASONS FOR ENTRY
TIME		
QUANTITY		
BUY PRICE		
SELL PRICE		
PROFIT (%)		
RISK REWARD		

WHAT I LEARNT FROM THIS TRADE		
WAS I IN THE CORRECT STATE OF MIND TO ENTER THIS TRADE?	Y	N
DID I USE POSITION SIZING PROPERLY?	Y	N
DID I FOLLOW ALL MY RULES?	Y	N
DID I REPEAT ANY OF MY OLD MISTAKES?	Y	N
AM I A BETTER TRADER THAN YESTERDAY?	Y	N

"It is better to fail in originality than to succeed in imitation."

REVIEW OF LAST 20 TRADES

Most successful strategy-

Worst performing strategy-

Best time for entry-

The Positives-

The Negatives-

DATE:

LOOKED FOR KEY SUPPORT &RESISTANCE LEVELS?	Y	N
ANALYSED YESTERDAY'S SESSION?	Y	N

		CHART ANALYSIS AND REASONS FOR ENTRY
TIME		
QUANTITY		
BUY PRICE		
SELL PRICE		
PROFIT (%)		
RISK REWARD		

WHAT I LEARNT FROM THIS TRADE		
WAS I IN THE CORRECT STATE OF MIND TO ENTER THIS TRADE?	Y	N
DID I USE POSITION SIZING PROPERLY?	Y	N
DID I FOLLOW ALL MY RULES?	Y	N
DID I REPEAT ANY OF MY OLD MISTAKES?	Y	N
AM I A BETTER TRADER THAN YESTERDAY?	Y	N

"Always remember, your focus determines your reality."

DATE:

LOOKED FOR KEY SUPPORT &RESISTANCE LEVELS?	Y	N
ANALYSED YESTERDAY'S SESSION?	Y	N

		CHART ANALYSIS AND REASONS FOR ENTRY
TIME		
QUANTITY		
BUY PRICE		
SELL PRICE		
PROFIT (%)		
RISK REWARD		

WHAT I LEARNT FROM THIS TRADE		
WAS I IN THE CORRECT STATE OF MIND TO ENTER THIS TRADE?	Y	N
DID I USE POSITION SIZING PROPERLY?	Y	N
DID I FOLLOW ALL MY RULES?	Y	N
DID I REPEAT ANY OF MY OLD MISTAKES?	Y	N
AM I A BETTER TRADER THAN YESTERDAY?	Y	N

"Success is walking from failure to failure with no loss of enthusiasm."

DATE:

LOOKED FOR KEY SUPPORT &RESISTANCE LEVELS?	Y	N
ANALYSED YESTERDAY'S SESSION?	Y	N

		CHART ANALYSIS AND REASONS FOR ENTRY
TIME		
QUANTITY		
BUY PRICE		
SELL PRICE		
PROFIT (%)		
RISK REWARD		

WHAT I LEARNT FROM THIS TRADE		
WAS I IN THE CORRECT STATE OF MIND TO ENTER THIS TRADE?	Y	N
DID I USE POSITION SIZING PROPERLY?	Y	N
DID I FOLLOW ALL MY RULES?	Y	N
DID I REPEAT ANY OF MY OLD MISTAKES?	Y	N
AM I A BETTER TRADER THAN YESTERDAY?	Y	N

"If you want to achieve excellence, you can get there today. As of this second, quit doing less-than-excellent work."

DATE:

LOOKED FOR KEY SUPPORT &RESISTANCE LEVELS?	Y	N
ANALYSED YESTERDAY'S SESSION?	Y	N

		CHART ANALYSIS AND REASONS FOR ENTRY
TIME		
QUANTITY		
BUY PRICE		
SELL PRICE		
PROFIT (%)		
RISK REWARD		

WHAT I LEARNT FROM THIS TRADE		

WAS I IN THE CORRECT STATE OF MIND TO ENTER THIS TRADE?	Y	N
DID I USE POSITION SIZING PROPERLY?	Y	N
DID I FOLLOW ALL MY RULES?	Y	N
DID I REPEAT ANY OF MY OLD MISTAKES?	Y	N
AM I A BETTER TRADER THAN YESTERDAY?	Y	N

"Before anything else, preparation is the key to success."

DATE:

LOOKED FOR KEY SUPPORT &RESISTANCE LEVELS?	Y	N
ANALYSED YESTERDAY'S SESSION?	Y	N

		CHART ANALYSIS AND REASONS FOR ENTRY
TIME		
QUANTITY		
BUY PRICE		
SELL PRICE		
PROFIT (%)		
RISK REWARD		

WHAT I LEARNT FROM THIS TRADE

WAS I IN THE CORRECT STATE OF MIND TO ENTER THIS TRADE?	Y	N
DID I USE POSITION SIZING PROPERLY?	Y	N
DID I FOLLOW ALL MY RULES?	Y	N
DID I REPEAT ANY OF MY OLD MISTAKES?	Y	N
AM I A BETTER TRADER THAN YESTERDAY?	Y	N

"The question isn't who is going to let me; it's who is going to stop me."

DATE:

LOOKED FOR KEY SUPPORT &RESISTANCE LEVELS?	Y	N
ANALYSED YESTERDAY'S SESSION?	Y	N

		CHART ANALYSIS AND REASONS FOR ENTRY
TIME		
QUANTITY		
BUY PRICE		
SELL PRICE		
PROFIT (%)		
RISK REWARD		

WHAT I LEARNT FROM THIS TRADE		
WAS I IN THE CORRECT STATE OF MIND TO ENTER THIS TRADE?	Y	N
DID I USE POSITION SIZING PROPERLY?	Y	N
DID I FOLLOW ALL MY RULES?	Y	N
DID I REPEAT ANY OF MY OLD MISTAKES?	Y	N
AM I A BETTER TRADER THAN YESTERDAY?	Y	N

"Everything you've ever wanted is on the other side of fear."

DATE:

LOOKED FOR KEY SUPPORT &RESISTANCE LEVELS?	Y	N
ANALYSED YESTERDAY'S SESSION?	Y	N

		CHART ANALYSIS AND REASONS FOR ENTRY
TIME		
QUANTITY		
BUY PRICE		
SELL PRICE		
PROFIT (%)		
RISK REWARD		

WHAT I LEARNT FROM THIS TRADE		

WAS I IN THE CORRECT STATE OF MIND TO ENTER THIS TRADE?	Y	N
DID I USE POSITION SIZING PROPERLY?	Y	N
DID I FOLLOW ALL MY RULES?	Y	N
DID I REPEAT ANY OF MY OLD MISTAKES?	Y	N
AM I A BETTER TRADER THAN YESTERDAY?	Y	N

"It does not matter how slowly you go as long as you do not stop."

DATE:

LOOKED FOR KEY SUPPORT &RESISTANCE LEVELS?	Y	N
ANALYSED YESTERDAY'S SESSION?	Y	N

		CHART ANALYSIS AND REASONS FOR ENTRY
TIME		
QUANTITY		
BUY PRICE		
SELL PRICE		
PROFIT (%)		
RISK REWARD		

WHAT I LEARNT FROM THIS TRADE		

WAS I IN THE CORRECT STATE OF MIND TO ENTER THIS TRADE?	Y	N
DID I USE POSITION SIZING PROPERLY?	Y	N
DID I FOLLOW ALL MY RULES?	Y	N
DID I REPEAT ANY OF MY OLD MISTAKES?	Y	N
AM I A BETTER TRADER THAN YESTERDAY?	Y	N

"Don't let the fear of losing be greater than the excitement of winning."

DATE:

LOOKED FOR KEY SUPPORT &RESISTANCE LEVELS?	Y	N
ANALYSED YESTERDAY'S SESSION?	Y	N

TIME	
QUANTITY	
BUY PRICE	
SELL PRICE	
PROFIT (%)	
RISK REWARD	

CHART ANALYSIS AND REASONS FOR ENTRY

WHAT I LEARNT FROM THIS TRADE

WAS I IN THE CORRECT STATE OF MIND TO ENTER THIS TRADE?	Y	N
DID I USE POSITION SIZING PROPERLY?	Y	N
DID I FOLLOW ALL MY RULES?	Y	N
DID I REPEAT ANY OF MY OLD MISTAKES?	Y	N
AM I A BETTER TRADER THAN YESTERDAY?	Y	N

"Obstacles are those frightful things you see when you take your eyes off your goal."

DATE:

LOOKED FOR KEY SUPPORT &RESISTANCE LEVELS?	Y	N
ANALYSED YESTERDAY'S SESSION?	Y	N

TIME	
QUANTITY	
BUY PRICE	
SELL PRICE	
PROFIT (%)	
RISK REWARD	

CHART ANALYSIS AND REASONS FOR ENTRY

WHAT I LEARNT FROM THIS TRADE

WAS I IN THE CORRECT STATE OF MIND TO ENTER THIS TRADE?	Y	N
DID I USE POSITION SIZING PROPERLY?	Y	N
DID I FOLLOW ALL MY RULES?	Y	N
DID I REPEAT ANY OF MY OLD MISTAKES?	Y	N
AM I A BETTER TRADER THAN YESTERDAY?	Y	N

"Develop success from failures. Discouragement and failure are two of the surest stepping stones to success."

DATE:

LOOKED FOR KEY SUPPORT &RESISTANCE LEVELS?	Y	N
ANALYSED YESTERDAY'S SESSION?	Y	N

		CHART ANALYSIS AND REASONS FOR ENTRY
TIME		
QUANTITY		
BUY PRICE		
SELL PRICE		
PROFIT (%)		
RISK REWARD		

WHAT I LEARNT FROM THIS TRADE		

WAS I IN THE CORRECT STATE OF MIND TO ENTER THIS TRADE?	Y	N
DID I USE POSITION SIZING PROPERLY?	Y	N
DID I FOLLOW ALL MY RULES?	Y	N
DID I REPEAT ANY OF MY OLD MISTAKES?	Y	N
AM I A BETTER TRADER THAN YESTERDAY?	Y	N

"It is your determination and persistence that will make you a successful person."

DATE:

LOOKED FOR KEY SUPPORT &RESISTANCE LEVELS?	Y	N
ANALYSED YESTERDAY'S SESSION?	Y	N

		CHART ANALYSIS AND REASONS FOR ENTRY
TIME		
QUANTITY		
BUY PRICE		
SELL PRICE		
PROFIT (%)		
RISK REWARD		

WHAT I LEARNT FROM THIS TRADE		
WAS I IN THE CORRECT STATE OF MIND TO ENTER THIS TRADE?	Y	N
DID I USE POSITION SIZING PROPERLY?	Y	N
DID I FOLLOW ALL MY RULES?	Y	N
DID I REPEATE ANY OF MY OLD MISTAKES?	Y	N
AM I A BETTER TRADER THAN YESTERDAY?	Y	N

'The measure of intelligence is the ability to change'

DATE:

LOOKED FOR KEY SUPPORT &RESISTANCE LEVELS?	Y	N
ANALYSED YESTERDAY'S SESSION?	Y	N

		CHART ANALYSIS AND REASONS FOR ENTRY
TIME		
QUANTITY		
BUY PRICE		
SELL PRICE		
PROFIT (%)		
RISK REWARD		

WHAT I LEARNT FROM THIS TRADE		
WAS I IN THE CORRECT STATE OF MIND TO ENTER THIS TRADE?	Y	N
DID I USE POSITION SIZING PROPERLY?	Y	N
DID I FOLLOW ALL MY RULES?	Y	N
DID I REPEAT ANY OF MY OLD MISTAKES?	Y	N
AM I A BETTER TRADER THAN YESTERDAY?	Y	N

'The greatest discovery of all time is that a person can change his future by merely changing his attitude'

DATE:

LOOKED FOR KEY SUPPORT &RESISTANCE LEVELS?	Y	N
ANALYSED YESTERDAY'S SESSION?	Y	N

		CHART ANALYSIS AND REASONS FOR ENTRY
TIME		
QUANTITY		
BUY PRICE		
SELL PRICE		
PROFIT (%)		
RISK REWARD		

WHAT I LEARNT FROM THIS TRADE		
WAS I IN THE CORRECT STATE OF MIND TO ENTER THIS TRADE?	Y	N
DID I USE POSITION SIZING PROPERLY?	Y	N
DID I FOLLOW ALL MY RULES?	Y	N
DID I REPEAT ANY OF MY OLD MISTAKES?	Y	N
AM I A BETTER TRADER THAN YESTERDAY?	Y	N

'Everyone thinks of changing the world, but no one thinks of changing himself.'

DATE:

LOOKED FOR KEY SUPPORT &RESISTANCE LEVELS?	Y	N
ANALYSED YESTERDAY'S SESSION?	Y	N

TIME	
QUANTITY	
BUY PRICE	
SELL PRICE	
PROFIT (%)	
RISK REWARD	

CHART ANALYSIS AND REASONS FOR ENTRY

WHAT I LEARNT FROM THIS TRADE

WAS I IN THE CORRECT STATE OF MIND TO ENTER THIS TRADE?	Y	N
DID I USE POSITION SIZING PROPERLY?	Y	N
DID I FOLLOW ALL MY RULES?	Y	N
DID I REPEAT ANY OF MY OLD MISTAKES?	Y	N
AM I A BETTER TRADER THAN YESTERDAY?	Y	N

"I can't change the direction of the wind, but I can adjust my sails to always reach my destination."

DATE:

LOOKED FOR KEY SUPPORT &RESISTANCE LEVELS?	Y	N
ANALYSED YESTERDAY'S SESSION?	Y	N

		CHART ANALYSIS AND REASONS FOR ENTRY
TIME		
QUANTITY		
BUY PRICE		
SELL PRICE		
PROFIT (%)		
RISK REWARD		

WHAT I LEARNT FROM THIS TRADE		
WAS I IN THE CORRECT STATE OF MIND TO ENTER THIS TRADE?	Y	N
DID I USE POSITION SIZING PROPERLY?	Y	N
DID I FOLLOW ALL MY RULES?	Y	N
DID I REPEAT ANY OF MY OLD MISTAKES?	Y	N
AM I A BETTER TRADER THAN YESTERDAY?	Y	N

"What's dangerous is not to evolve."

DATE:

LOOKED FOR KEY SUPPORT &RESISTANCE LEVELS?	Y	N
ANALYSED YESTERDAY'S SESSION?	Y	N

		CHART ANALYSIS AND REASONS FOR ENTRY
TIME		
QUANTITY		
BUY PRICE		
SELL PRICE		
PROFIT (%)		
RISK REWARD		

WHAT I LEARNT FROM THIS TRADE

WAS I IN THE CORRECT STATE OF MIND TO ENTER THIS TRADE?	Y	N
DID I USE POSITION SIZING PROPERLY?	Y	N
DID I FOLLOW ALL MY RULES?	Y	N
DID I REPEAT ANY OF MY OLD MISTAKES?	Y	N
AM I A BETTER TRADER THAN YESTERDAY?	Y	N

"Today was good. Today was fun. Tomorrow is another one."

DATE:

LOOKED FOR KEY SUPPORT &RESISTANCE LEVELS?	Y	N
ANALYSED YESTERDAY'S SESSION?	Y	N

		CHART ANALYSIS AND REASONS FOR ENTRY
TIME		
QUANTITY		
BUY PRICE		
SELL PRICE		
PROFIT (%)		
RISK REWARD		

WHAT I LEARNT FROM THIS TRADE		

WAS I IN THE CORRECT STATE OF MIND TO ENTER THIS TRADE?	Y	N
DID I USE POSITION SIZING PROPERLY?	Y	N
DID I FOLLOW ALL MY RULES?	Y	N
DID I REPEAT ANY OF MY OLD MISTAKES?	Y	N
AM I A BETTER TRADER THAN YESTERDAY?	Y	N

"In order to design a future of positive change, we must first become expert at changing our minds."

DATE:

LOOKED FOR KEY SUPPORT &RESISTANCE LEVELS?	Y	N
ANALYSED YESTERDAY'S SESSION?	Y	N

TIME	
QUANTITY	
BUY PRICE	
SELL PRICE	
PROFIT (%)	
RISK REWARD	

CHART ANALYSIS AND REASONS FOR ENTRY

WHAT I LEARNT FROM THIS TRADE

WAS I IN THE CORRECT STATE OF MIND TO ENTER THIS TRADE?	Y	N
DID I USE POSITION SIZING PROPERLY?	Y	N
DID I FOLLOW ALL MY RULES?	Y	N
DID I REPEAT ANY OF MY OLD MISTAKES?	Y	N
AM I A BETTER TRADER THAN YESTERDAY?	Y	N

"Times and conditions change so rapidly that we must keep our aim constantly focused on the future."

DATE:

LOOKED FOR KEY SUPPORT &RESISTANCE LEVELS?	Y	N
ANALYSED YESTERDAY'S SESSION?	Y	N

		CHART ANALYSIS AND REASONS FOR ENTRY
TIME		
QUANTITY		
BUY PRICE		
SELL PRICE		
PROFIT (%)		
RISK REWARD		

WHAT I LEARNT FROM THIS TRADE		

WAS I IN THE CORRECT STATE OF MIND TO ENTER THIS TRADE?	Y	N
DID I USE POSITION SIZING PROPERLY?	Y	N
DID I FOLLOW ALL MY RULES?	Y	N
DID I REPEAT ANY OF MY OLD MISTAKES?	Y	N
AM I A BETTER TRADER THAN YESTERDAY?	Y	N

"Anyone who has never made a mistake has never tried anything new."

DATE:

REVIEW OF LAST 20 TRADES
Most successful strategy-
Worst performing strategy-
Best time for entry-
The Positives-
The Negatives-

DATE:

LOOKED FOR KEY SUPPORT &RESISTANCE LEVELS?	Y	N
ANALYSED YESTERDAY'S SESSION?	Y	N

TIME	
QUANTITY	
BUY PRICE	
SELL PRICE	
PROFIT (%)	
RISK REWARD	

CHART ANALYSIS AND REASONS FOR ENTRY

WHAT I LEARNT FROM THIS TRADE

WAS I IN THE CORRECT STATE OF MIND TO ENTER THIS TRADE?	Y	N
DID I USE POSITION SIZING PROPERLY?	Y	N
DID I FOLLOW ALL MY RULES?	Y	N
DID I REPEAT ANY OF MY OLD MISTAKES?	Y	N
AM I A BETTER TRADER THAN YESTERDAY?	Y	N

"Knowing what must be done does away with fear."

DATE:

LOOKED FOR KEY SUPPORT &RESISTANCE LEVELS?	Y	N
ANALYSED YESTERDAY'S SESSION?	Y	N

		CHART ANALYSIS AND REASONS FOR ENTRY
TIME		
QUANTITY		
BUY PRICE		
SELL PRICE		
PROFIT (%)		
RISK REWARD		

WHAT I LEARNT FROM THIS TRADE		
WAS I IN THE CORRECT STATE OF MIND TO ENTER THIS TRADE?	Y	N
DID I USE POSITION SIZING PROPERLY?	Y	N
DID I FOLLOW ALL MY RULES?	Y	N
DID I REPEAT ANY OF MY OLD MISTAKES?	Y	N
AM I A BETTER TRADER THAN YESTERDAY?	Y	N

"We don't see things the way they are. We see them the way we are."

DATE:

LOOKED FOR KEY SUPPORT &RESISTANCE LEVELS?	Y	N
ANALYSED YESTERDAY'S SESSION?	Y	N

TIME	
QUANTITY	
BUY PRICE	
SELL PRICE	
PROFIT (%)	
RISK REWARD	

CHART ANALYSIS AND REASONS FOR ENTRY

WHAT I LEARNT FROM THIS TRADE

WAS I IN THE CORRECT STATE OF MIND TO ENTER THIS TRADE?	Y	N
DID I USE POSITION SIZING PROPERLY?	Y	N
DID I FOLLOW ALL MY RULES?	Y	N
DID I REPEAT ANY OF MY OLD MISTAKES?	Y	N
AM I A BETTER TRADER THAN YESTERDAY?	Y	N

"Learn from the mistakes of others. You can't live long enough to make them all yourself."

DATE:

LOOKED FOR KEY SUPPORT &RESISTANCE LEVELS?	Y	N
ANALYSED YESTERDAY'S SESSION?	Y	N

		CHART ANALYSIS AND REASONS FOR ENTRY
TIME		
QUANTITY		
BUY PRICE		
SELL PRICE		
PROFIT (%)		
RISK REWARD		

WHAT I LEARNT FROM THIS TRADE		
WAS I IN THE CORRECT STATE OF MIND TO ENTER THIS TRADE?	Y	N
DID I USE POSITION SIZING PROPERLY?	Y	N
DID I FOLLOW ALL MY RULES?	Y	N
DID I REPEAT ANY OF MY OLD MISTAKES?	Y	N
AM I A BETTER TRADER THAN YESTERDAY?	Y	N

"The only thing standing between you and outrageous success is continuous progress."

DATE:

LOOKED FOR KEY SUPPORT &RESISTANCE LEVELS?	Y	N
ANALYSED YESTERDAY'S SESSION?	Y	N

		CHART ANALYSIS AND REASONS FOR ENTRY
TIME		
QUANTITY		
BUY PRICE		
SELL PRICE		
PROFIT (%)		
RISK REWARD		

WHAT I LEARNT FROM THIS TRADE		
WAS I IN THE CORRECT STATE OF MIND TO ENTER THIS TRADE?	Y	N
DID I USE POSITION SIZING PROPERLY?	Y	N
DID I FOLLOW ALL MY RULES?	Y	N
DID I REPEAT ANY OF MY OLD MISTAKES?	Y	N
AM I A BETTER TRADER THAN YESTERDAY?	Y	N

"Setting goals is the first step in turning the invisible into the visible."

DATE:

LOOKED FOR KEY SUPPORT &RESISTANCE LEVELS?	Y	N
ANALYSED YESTERDAY'S SESSION?	Y	N

		CHART ANALYSIS AND REASONS FOR ENTRY
TIME		
QUANTITY		
BUY PRICE		
SELL PRICE		
PROFIT (%)		
RISK REWARD		

WHAT I LEARNT FROM THIS TRADE		
WAS I IN THE CORRECT STATE OF MIND TO ENTER THIS TRADE?	Y	N
DID I USE POSITION SIZING PROPERLY?	Y	N
DID I FOLLOW ALL MY RULES?	Y	N
DID I REPEAT ANY OF MY OLD MISTAKES?	Y	N
AM I A BETTER TRADER THAN YESTERDAY?	Y	N

"Talent is cheaper than table salt. What separates the talented individual from the successful one is a lot of hard work."

DATE:

LOOKED FOR KEY SUPPORT &RESISTANCE LEVELS?	Y	N
ANALYSED YESTERDAY'S SESSION?	Y	N

		CHART ANALYSIS AND REASONS FOR ENTRY
TIME		
QUANTITY		
BUY PRICE		
SELL PRICE		
PROFIT (%)		
RISK REWARD		

WHAT I LEARNT FROM THIS TRADE		
WAS I IN THE CORRECT STATE OF MIND TO ENTER THIS TRADE?	Y	N
DID I USE POSITION SIZING PROPERLY?	Y	N
DID I FOLLOW ALL MY RULES?	Y	N
DID I REPEAT ANY OF MY OLD MISTAKES?	Y	N
AM I A BETTER TRADER THAN YESTERDAY?	Y	N

"Impossible is just an opinion."

DATE:

LOOKED FOR KEY SUPPORT &RESISTANCE LEVELS?	Y	N
ANALYSED YESTERDAY'S SESSION?	Y	N

TIME	
QUANTITY	
BUY PRICE	
SELL PRICE	
PROFIT (%)	
RISK REWARD	

CHART ANALYSIS AND REASONS FOR ENTRY

WHAT I LEARNT FROM THIS TRADE

WAS I IN THE CORRECT STATE OF MIND TO ENTER THIS TRADE?	Y	N
DID I USE POSITION SIZING PROPERLY?	Y	N
DID I FOLLOW ALL MY RULES?	Y	N
DID I REPEAT ANY OF MY OLD MISTAKES?	Y	N
AM I A BETTER TRADER THAN YESTERDAY?	Y	N

"You are your greatest asset. Put your time, effort, and money into training."

DATE:

LOOKED FOR KEY SUPPORT &RESISTANCE LEVELS?	Y	N
ANALYSED YESTERDAY'S SESSION?	Y	N

TIME	
QUANTITY	
BUY PRICE	
SELL PRICE	
PROFIT (%)	
RISK REWARD	

CHART ANALYSIS AND REASONS FOR ENTRY

WHAT I LEARNT FROM THIS TRADE

WAS I IN THE CORRECT STATE OF MIND TO ENTER THIS TRADE?	Y	N
DID I USE POSITION SIZING PROPERLY?	Y	N
DID I FOLLOW ALL MY RULES?	Y	N
DID I REPEAT ANY OF MY OLD MISTAKES?	Y	N
AM I A BETTER TRADER THAN YESTERDAY?	Y	N

"It's hard to beat a person who never gives up."

DATE:

LOOKED FOR KEY SUPPORT &RESISTANCE LEVELS?	Y	N
ANALYSED YESTERDAY'S SESSION?	Y	N

TIME	
QUANTITY	
BUY PRICE	
SELL PRICE	
PROFIT (%)	
RISK REWARD	

CHART ANALYSIS AND REASONS FOR ENTRY

WHAT I LEARNT FROM THIS TRADE

WAS I IN THE CORRECT STATE OF MIND TO ENTER THIS TRADE?	Y	N
DID I USE POSITION SIZING PROPERLY?	Y	N
DID I FOLLOW ALL MY RULES?	Y	N
DID I REPEAT ANY OF MY OLD MISTAKES?	Y	N
AM I A BETTER TRADER THAN YESTERDAY?	Y	N

"Do or do not. There is no try."

DATE:

<table>
<tr><td>LOOKED FOR KEY SUPPORT &RESISTANCE LEVELS?</td><td>Y</td><td>N</td></tr>
<tr><td>ANALYSED YESTERDAY'S SESSION?</td><td>Y</td><td>N</td></tr>
</table>

TIME		CHART ANALYSIS AND REASONS FOR ENTRY
QUANTITY		
BUY PRICE		
SELL PRICE		
PROFIT (%)		
RISK REWARD		

WHAT I LEARNT FROM THIS TRADE

<table>
<tr><td>WAS I IN THE CORRECT STATE OF MIND TO ENTER THIS TRADE?</td><td>Y</td><td>N</td></tr>
<tr><td>DID I USE POSITION SIZING PROPERLY?</td><td>Y</td><td>N</td></tr>
<tr><td>DID I FOLLOW ALL MY RULES?</td><td>Y</td><td>N</td></tr>
<tr><td>DID I REPEAT ANY OF MY OLD MISTAKES?</td><td>Y</td><td>N</td></tr>
<tr><td>AM I A BETTER TRADER THAN YESTERDAY?</td><td>Y</td><td>N</td></tr>
</table>

"Doing the best at this moment puts you in the best place for the next moment."

DATE:

LOOKED FOR KEY SUPPORT &RESISTANCE LEVELS?	Y	N
ANALYSED YESTERDAY'S SESSION?	Y	N

		CHART ANALYSIS AND REASONS FOR ENTRY
TIME		
QUANTITY		
BUY PRICE		
SELL PRICE		
PROFIT (%)		
RISK REWARD		

WHAT I LEARNT FROM THIS TRADE		
WAS I IN THE CORRECT STATE OF MIND TO ENTER THIS TRADE?	Y	N
DID I USE POSITION SIZING PROPERLY?	Y	N
DID I FOLLOW ALL MY RULES?	Y	N
DID I REPEAT ANY OF MY OLD MISTAKES?	Y	N
AM I A BETTER TRADER THAN YESTERDAY?	Y	N

"Obstacles can't stop you. Problems can't stop you. Most of all, other people can't stop you. Only you can stop you."

DATE:

LOOKED FOR KEY SUPPORT &RESISTANCE LEVELS?	Y	N
ANALYSED YESTERDAY'S SESSION?	Y	N

TIME	
QUANTITY	
BUY PRICE	
SELL PRICE	
PROFIT (%)	
RISK REWARD	

CHART ANALYSIS AND REASONS FOR ENTRY

WHAT I LEARNT FROM THIS TRADE

WAS I IN THE CORRECT STATE OF MIND TO ENTER THIS TRADE?	Y	N
DID I USE POSITION SIZING PROPERLY?	Y	N
DID I FOLLOW ALL MY RULES?	Y	N
DID I REPEAT ANY OF MY OLD MISTAKES?	Y	N
AM I A BETTER TRADER THAN YESTERDAY?	Y	N

"*Most important things in the world have been accomplished by people who have kept on trying when there seemed to be no hope at all.*"

DATE:

LOOKED FOR KEY SUPPORT &RESISTANCE LEVELS?	Y	N
ANALYSED YESTERDAY'S SESSION?	Y	N

		CHART ANALYSIS AND REASONS FOR ENTRY
TIME		
QUANTITY		
BUY PRICE		
SELL PRICE		
PROFIT (%)		
RISK REWARD		

WHAT I LEARNT FROM THIS TRADE		
WAS I IN THE CORRECT STATE OF MIND TO ENTER THIS TRADE?	Y	N
DID I USE POSITION SIZING PROPERLY?	Y	N
DID I FOLLOW ALL MY RULES?	Y	N
DID I REPEAT ANY OF MY OLD MISTAKES?	Y	N
AM I A BETTER TRADER THAN YESTERDAY?	Y	N

"The harder the conflict, the more glorious the triumph."

DATE:

LOOKED FOR KEY SUPPORT &RESISTANCE LEVELS?	Y	N
ANALYSED YESTERDAY'S SESSION?	Y	N

		CHART ANALYSIS AND REASONS FOR ENTRY
TIME		
QUANTITY		
BUY PRICE		
SELL PRICE		
PROFIT (%)		
RISK REWARD		

WHAT I LEARNT FROM THIS TRADE		
WAS I IN THE CORRECT STATE OF MIND TO ENTER THIS TRADE?	Y	N
DID I USE POSITION SIZING PROPERLY?	Y	N
DID I FOLLOW ALL MY RULES?	Y	N
DID I REPEAT ANY OF MY OLD MISTAKES?	Y	N
AM I A BETTER TRADER THAN YESTERDAY?	Y	N

"Perseverance is not a long race; it is many short races one after the other."

DATE:

LOOKED FOR KEY SUPPORT &RESISTANCE LEVELS?	Y	N
ANALYSED YESTERDAY'S SESSION?	Y	N

		CHART ANALYSIS AND REASONS FOR ENTRY
TIME		
QUANTITY		
BUY PRICE		
SELL PRICE		
PROFIT (%)		
RISK REWARD		

WHAT I LEARNT FROM THIS TRADE		
WAS I IN THE CORRECT STATE OF MIND TO ENTER THIS TRADE?	Y	N
DID I USE POSITION SIZING PROPERLY?	Y	N
DID I FOLLOW ALL MY RULES?	Y	N
DID I REPEAT ANY OF MY OLD MISTAKES?	Y	N
AM I A BETTER TRADER THAN YESTERDAY?	Y	N

"Success is the sum of small efforts, repeated day in and day out."

DATE:

LOOKED FOR KEY SUPPORT &RESISTANCE LEVELS?	Y	N
ANALYSED YESTERDAY'S SESSION?	Y	N

		CHART ANALYSIS AND REASONS FOR ENTRY
TIME		
QUANTITY		
BUY PRICE		
SELL PRICE		
PROFIT (%)		
RISK REWARD		

WHAT I LEARNT FROM THIS TRADE		
WAS I IN THE CORRECT STATE OF MIND TO ENTER THIS TRADE?	Y	N
DID I USE POSITION SIZING PROPERLY?	Y	N
DID I FOLLOW ALL MY RULES?	Y	N
DID I REPEAT ANY OF MY OLD MISTAKES?	Y	N
AM I A BETTER TRADER THAN YESTERDAY?	Y	N

"Never confuse a single defeat with a final defeat."

DATE:

LOOKED FOR KEY SUPPORT &RESISTANCE LEVELS?	Y	N
ANALYSED YESTERDAY'S SESSION?	Y	N

		CHART ANALYSIS AND REASONS FOR ENTRY
TIME		
QUANTITY		
BUY PRICE		
SELL PRICE		
PROFIT (%)		
RISK REWARD		

WHAT I LEARNT FROM THIS TRADE		

WAS I IN THE CORRECT STATE OF MIND TO ENTER THIS TRADE?	Y	N
DID I USE POSITION SIZING PROPERLY?	Y	N
DID I FOLLOW ALL MY RULES?	Y	N
DID I REPEAT ANY OF MY OLD MISTAKES?	Y	N
AM I A BETTER TRADER THAN YESTERDAY?	Y	N

"It's so freeing, it's beautiful in a way, to have a great failure, there's nowhere to go but up."

DATE:

LOOKED FOR KEY SUPPORT &RESISTANCE LEVELS?	Y	N
ANALYSED YESTERDAY'S SESSION?	Y	N

		CHART ANALYSIS AND REASONS FOR ENTRY
TIME		
QUANTITY		
BUY PRICE		
SELL PRICE		
PROFIT (%)		
RISK REWARD		

WHAT I LEARNT FROM THIS TRADE		
WAS I IN THE CORRECT STATE OF MIND TO ENTER THIS TRADE?	Y	N
DID I USE POSITION SIZING PROPERLY?	Y	N
DID I FOLLOW ALL MY RULES?	Y	N
DID I REPEAT ANY OF MY OLD MISTAKES?	Y	N
AM I A BETTER TRADER THAN YESTERDAY?	Y	N

"You may be the only person left who believes in you, but it's enough. It takes just one star to pierce a universe of darkness. Never give up."

DATE:

LOOKED FOR KEY SUPPORT &RESISTANCE LEVELS?	Y	N
ANALYSED YESTERDAY'S SESSION?	Y	N

		CHART ANALYSIS AND REASONS FOR ENTRY
TIME		
QUANTITY		
BUY PRICE		
SELL PRICE		
PROFIT (%)		
RISK REWARD		

WHAT I LEARNT FROM THIS TRADE		
WAS I IN THE CORRECT STATE OF MIND TO ENTER THIS TRADE?	Y	N
DID I USE POSITION SIZING PROPERLY?	Y	N
DID I FOLLOW ALL MY RULES?	Y	N
DID I REPEAT ANY OF MY OLD MISTAKES?	Y	N
AM I A BETTER TRADER THAN YESTERDAY?	Y	N

"Don't judge each day by the harvest you reap but by the seeds that you plant."

DATE:

REVIEW OF LAST 20 TRADES
Most successful strategy-
Worst performing strategy-
Best time for entry-
The Positives-
The Negatives-

DATE:

LOOKED FOR KEY SUPPORT &RESISTANCE LEVELS?	Y	N
ANALYSED YESTERDAY'S SESSION?	Y	N

		CHART ANALYSIS AND REASONS FOR ENTRY
TIME		
QUANTITY		
BUY PRICE		
SELL PRICE		
PROFIT (%)		
RISK REWARD		

WHAT I LEARNT FROM THIS TRADE		
WAS I IN THE CORRECT STATE OF MIND TO ENTER THIS TRADE?	Y	N
DID I USE POSITION SIZING PROPERLY?	Y	N
DID I FOLLOW ALL MY RULES?	Y	N
DID I REPEAT ANY OF MY OLD MISTAKES?	Y	N
AM I A BETTER TRADER THAN YESTERDAY?	Y	N

"Happiness is not in the mere possession of money; it lies in the joy of achievement, in the thrill of creative effort."

DATE:

LOOKED FOR KEY SUPPORT &RESISTANCE LEVELS?	Y	N
ANALYSED YESTERDAY'S SESSION?	Y	N

		CHART ANALYSIS AND REASONS FOR ENTRY
TIME		
QUANTITY		
BUY PRICE		
SELL PRICE		
PROFIT (%)		
RISK REWARD		

WHAT I LEARNT FROM THIS TRADE		
WAS I IN THE CORRECT STATE OF MIND TO ENTER THIS TRADE?	Y	N
DID I USE POSITION SIZING PROPERLY?	Y	N
DID I FOLLOW ALL MY RULES?	Y	N
DID I REPEAT ANY OF MY OLD MISTAKES?	Y	N
AM I A BETTER TRADER THAN YESTERDAY?	Y	N

"There is always light. If only we're brave enough to see it. If only we're brave enough to be it."

DATE:

LOOKED FOR KEY SUPPORT &RESISTANCE LEVELS?	Y	N
ANALYSED YESTERDAY'S SESSION?	Y	N

		CHART ANALYSIS AND REASONS FOR ENTRY
TIME		
QUANTITY		
BUY PRICE		
SELL PRICE		
PROFIT (%)		
RISK REWARD		

WHAT I LEARNT FROM THIS TRADE		
WAS I IN THE CORRECT STATE OF MIND TO ENTER THIS TRADE?	Y	N
DID I USE POSITION SIZING PROPERLY?	Y	N
DID I FOLLOW ALL MY RULES?	Y	N
DID I REPEATE ANY OF MY OLD MISTAKES?	Y	N
AM I A BETTER TRADER THAN YESTERDAY?	Y	N

"Nobody who ever gave his best regretted it."

DATE:

LOOKED FOR KEY SUPPORT &RESISTANCE LEVELS?	Y	N
ANALYSED YESTERDAY'S SESSION?	Y	N

		CHART ANALYSIS AND REASONS FOR ENTRY
TIME		
QUANTITY		
BUY PRICE		
SELL PRICE		
PROFIT (%)		
RISK REWARD		

WHAT I LEARNT FROM THIS TRADE		
WAS I IN THE CORRECT STATE OF MIND TO ENTER THIS TRADE?	Y	N
DID I USE POSITION SIZING PROPERLY?	Y	N
DID I FOLLOW ALL MY RULES?	Y	N
DID I REPEAT ANY OF MY OLD MISTAKES?	Y	N
AM I A BETTER TRADER THAN YESTERDAY?	Y	N

"Education is not the learning of the facts, but the training of the mind to think."

DATE:

LOOKED FOR KEY SUPPORT &RESISTANCE LEVELS?	Y	N
ANALYSED YESTERDAY'S SESSION?	Y	N

		CHART ANALYSIS AND REASONS FOR ENTRY
TIME		
QUANTITY		
BUY PRICE		
SELL PRICE		
PROFIT (%)		
RISK REWARD		

WHAT I LEARNT FROM THIS TRADE		
WAS I IN THE CORRECT STATE OF MIND TO ENTER THIS TRADE?	Y	N
DID I USE POSITION SIZING PROPERLY?	Y	N
DID I FOLLOW ALL MY RULES?	Y	N
DID I REPEAT ANY OF MY OLD MISTAKES?	Y	N
AM I A BETTER TRADER THAN YESTERDAY?	Y	N

"If you surrender to the wind, you can ride it."

DATE:

LOOKED FOR KEY SUPPORT &RESISTANCE LEVELS?	Y	N
ANALYSED YESTERDAY'S SESSION?	Y	N

		CHART ANALYSIS AND REASONS FOR ENTRY
TIME		
QUANTITY		
BUY PRICE		
SELL PRICE		
PROFIT (%)		
RISK REWARD		

WHAT I LEARNT FROM THIS TRADE		
WAS I IN THE CORRECT STATE OF MIND TO ENTER THIS TRADE?	Y	N
DID I USE POSITION SIZING PROPERLY?	Y	N
DID I FOLLOW ALL MY RULES?	Y	N
DID I REPEAT ANY OF MY OLD MISTAKES?	Y	N
AM I A BETTER TRADER THAN YESTERDAY?	Y	N

"We don't see things the way they are. We see them the way we are."

DATE:

LOOKED FOR KEY SUPPORT &RESISTANCE LEVELS?	Y	N
ANALYSED YESTERDAY'S SESSION?	Y	N

		CHART ANALYSIS AND REASONS FOR ENTRY
TIME		
QUANTITY		
BUY PRICE		
SELL PRICE		
PROFIT (%)		
RISK REWARD		

WHAT I LEARNT FROM THIS TRADE		
WAS I IN THE CORRECT STATE OF MIND TO ENTER THIS TRADE?	Y	N
DID I USE POSITION SIZING PROPERLY?	Y	N
DID I FOLLOW ALL MY RULES?	Y	N
DID I REPEAT ANY OF MY OLD MISTAKES?	Y	N
AM I A BETTER TRADER THAN YESTERDAY?	Y	N

"Many receive advice, only the wise profit from it."

DATE:

LOOKED FOR KEY SUPPORT &RESISTANCE LEVELS?	Y	N
ANALYSED YESTERDAY'S SESSION?	Y	N

		CHART ANALYSIS AND REASONS FOR ENTRY
TIME		
QUANTITY		
BUY PRICE		
SELL PRICE		
PROFIT (%)		
RISK REWARD		

WHAT I LEARNT FROM THIS TRADE		
WAS I IN THE CORRECT STATE OF MIND TO ENTER THIS TRADE?	Y	N
DID I USE POSITION SIZING PROPERLY?	Y	N
DID I FOLLOW ALL MY RULES?	Y	N
DID I REPEAT ANY OF MY OLD MISTAKES?	Y	N
AM I A BETTER TRADER THAN YESTERDAY?	Y	N

"Our greatest glory is not in never falling, but in rising every time we fall."

DATE:

LOOKED FOR KEY SUPPORT &RESISTANCE LEVELS?	Y	N
ANALYSED YESTERDAY'S SESSION?	Y	N

TIME	
QUANTITY	
BUY PRICE	
SELL PRICE	
PROFIT (%)	
RISK REWARD	

CHART ANALYSIS AND REASONS FOR ENTRY

WHAT I LEARNT FROM THIS TRADE

WAS I IN THE CORRECT STATE OF MIND TO ENTER THIS TRADE?	Y	N
DID I USE POSITION SIZING PROPERLY?	Y	N
DID I FOLLOW ALL MY RULES?	Y	N
DID I REPEAT ANY OF MY OLD MISTAKES?	Y	N
AM I A BETTER TRADER THAN YESTERDAY?	Y	N

"Energy and persistence conquer all things."

DATE:

LOOKED FOR KEY SUPPORT &RESISTANCE LEVELS?	Y	N
ANALYSED YESTERDAY'S SESSION?	Y	N

		CHART ANALYSIS AND REASONS FOR ENTRY
TIME		
QUANTITY		
BUY PRICE		
SELL PRICE		
PROFIT (%)		
RISK REWARD		

WHAT I LEARNT FROM THIS TRADE		
WAS I IN THE CORRECT STATE OF MIND TO ENTER THIS TRADE?	Y	N
DID I USE POSITION SIZING PROPERLY?	Y	N
DID I FOLLOW ALL MY RULES?	Y	N
DID I REPEAT ANY OF MY OLD MISTAKES?	Y	N
AM I A BETTER TRADER THAN YESTERDAY?	Y	N

"Ambition is the path to success. Persistence is the vehicle you arrive in."

DATE:

LOOKED FOR KEY SUPPORT &RESISTANCE LEVELS?	Y	N
ANALYSED YESTERDAY'S SESSION?	Y	N

TIME	
QUANTITY	
BUY PRICE	
SELL PRICE	
PROFIT (%)	
RISK REWARD	

CHART ANALYSIS AND REASONS FOR ENTRY

WHAT I LEARNT FROM THIS TRADE

WAS I IN THE CORRECT STATE OF MIND TO ENTER THIS TRADE?	Y	N
DID I USE POSITION SIZING PROPERLY?	Y	N
DID I FOLLOW ALL MY RULES?	Y	N
DID I REPEAT ANY OF MY OLD MISTAKES?	Y	N
AM I A BETTER TRADER THAN YESTERDAY?	Y	N

"The future depends on what you do today."

DATE:

LOOKED FOR KEY SUPPORT &RESISTANCE LEVELS?	Y	N
ANALYSED YESTERDAY'S SESSION?	Y	N

		CHART ANALYSIS AND REASONS FOR ENTRY
TIME		
QUANTITY		
BUY PRICE		
SELL PRICE		
PROFIT (%)		
RISK REWARD		

WHAT I LEARNT FROM THIS TRADE		
WAS I IN THE CORRECT STATE OF MIND TO ENTER THIS TRADE?	Y	N
DID I USE POSITION SIZING PROPERLY?	Y	N
DID I FOLLOW ALL MY RULES?	Y	N
DID I REPEAT ANY OF MY OLD MISTAKES?	Y	N
AM I A BETTER TRADER THAN YESTERDAY?	Y	N

"Believe in yourself, push your limits, experience life, conquer your goals, and be happy."

DATE:

		Y	N
LOOKED FOR KEY SUPPORT &RESISTANCE LEVELS?		Y	N
ANALYSED YESTERDAY'S SESSION?		Y	N

		CHART ANALYSIS AND REASONS FOR ENTRY
TIME		
QUANTITY		
BUY PRICE		
SELL PRICE		
PROFIT (%)		
RISK REWARD		

WHAT I LEARNT FROM THIS TRADE		
WAS I IN THE CORRECT STATE OF MIND TO ENTER THIS TRADE?	Y	N
DID I USE POSITION SIZING PROPERLY?	Y	N
DID I FOLLOW ALL MY RULES?	Y	N
DID I REPEAT ANY OF MY OLD MISTAKES?	Y	N
AM I A BETTER TRADER THAN YESTERDAY?	Y	N

"It's no use going back to yesterday because I was a different person then."

DATE:

LOOKED FOR KEY SUPPORT &RESISTANCE LEVELS?	Y	N
ANALYSED YESTERDAY'S SESSION?	Y	N

		CHART ANALYSIS AND REASONS FOR ENTRY
TIME		
QUANTITY		
BUY PRICE		
SELL PRICE		
PROFIT (%)		
RISK REWARD		

WHAT I LEARNT FROM THIS TRADE		
WAS I IN THE CORRECT STATE OF MIND TO ENTER THIS TRADE?	Y	N
DID I USE POSITION SIZING PROPERLY?	Y	N
DID I FOLLOW ALL MY RULES?	Y	N
DID I REPEAT ANY OF MY OLD MISTAKES?	Y	N
AM I A BETTER TRADER THAN YESTERDAY?	Y	N

"There are no secrets to success. It is the result of preparation, hard work, and learning from failure."

DATE:

LOOKED FOR KEY SUPPORT &RESISTANCE LEVELS?	Y	N
ANALYSED YESTERDAY'S SESSION?	Y	N

		CHART ANALYSIS AND REASONS FOR ENTRY
TIME		
QUANTITY		
BUY PRICE		
SELL PRICE		
PROFIT (%)		
RISK REWARD		

WHAT I LEARNT FROM THIS TRADE		
WAS I IN THE CORRECT STATE OF MIND TO ENTER THIS TRADE?	Y	N
DID I USE POSITION SIZING PROPERLY?	Y	N
DID I FOLLOW ALL MY RULES?	Y	N
DID I REPEAT ANY OF MY OLD MISTAKES?	Y	N
AM I A BETTER TRADER THAN YESTERDAY?	Y	N

"Success isn't always about greatness. It's about consistency. Consistent hard work leads to success. Greatness will come."

DATE:

LOOKED FOR KEY SUPPORT &RESISTANCE LEVELS?	Y	N
ANALYSED YESTERDAY'S SESSION?	Y	N

		CHART ANALYSIS AND REASONS FOR ENTRY
TIME		
QUANTITY		
BUY PRICE		
SELL PRICE		
PROFIT (%)		
RISK REWARD		

WHAT I LEARNT FROM THIS TRADE

WAS I IN THE CORRECT STATE OF MIND TO ENTER THIS TRADE?	Y	N
DID I USE POSITION SIZING PROPERLY?	Y	N
DID I FOLLOW ALL MY RULES?	Y	N
DID I REPEAT ANY OF MY OLD MISTAKES?	Y	N
AM I A BETTER TRADER THAN YESTERDAY?	Y	N

"Champions keep playing until they get it right."

DATE:

LOOKED FOR KEY SUPPORT &RESISTANCE LEVELS?	Y	N
ANALYSED YESTERDAY'S SESSION?	Y	N

		CHART ANALYSIS AND REASONS FOR ENTRY
TIME		
QUANTITY		
BUY PRICE		
SELL PRICE		
PROFIT (%)		
RISK REWARD		

WHAT I LEARNT FROM THIS TRADE		
WAS I IN THE CORRECT STATE OF MIND TO ENTER THIS TRADE?	Y	N
DID I USE POSITION SIZING PROPERLY?	Y	N
DID I FOLLOW ALL MY RULES?	Y	N
DID I REPEAT ANY OF MY OLD MISTAKES?	Y	N
AM I A BETTER TRADER THAN YESTERDAY?	Y	N

"It is during our darkest moments that we must focus to see the light."

DATE:

LOOKED FOR KEY SUPPORT &RESISTANCE LEVELS?	Y	N
ANALYSED YESTERDAY'S SESSION?	Y	N

		CHART ANALYSIS AND REASONS FOR ENTRY
TIME		
QUANTITY		
BUY PRICE		
SELL PRICE		
PROFIT (%)		
RISK REWARD		

WHAT I LEARNT FROM THIS TRADE		
WAS I IN THE CORRECT STATE OF MIND TO ENTER THIS TRADE?	Y	N
DID I USE POSITION SIZING PROPERLY?	Y	N
DID I FOLLOW ALL MY RULES?	Y	N
DID I REPEAT ANY OF MY OLD MISTAKES?	Y	N
AM I A BETTER TRADER THAN YESTERDAY?	Y	N

"Real change, enduring change, happens one step at a time."

DATE:

LOOKED FOR KEY SUPPORT &RESISTANCE LEVELS?	Y	N
ANALYSED YESTERDAY'S SESSION?	Y	N

TIME	
QUANTITY	
BUY PRICE	
SELL PRICE	
PROFIT (%)	
RISK REWARD	

CHART ANALYSIS AND REASONS FOR ENTRY

WHAT I LEARNT FROM THIS TRADE

WAS I IN THE CORRECT STATE OF MIND TO ENTER THIS TRADE?	Y	N
DID I USE POSITION SIZING PROPERLY?	Y	N
DID I FOLLOW ALL MY RULES?	Y	N
DID I REPEAT ANY OF MY OLD MISTAKES?	Y	N
AM I A BETTER TRADER THAN YESTERDAY?	Y	N

"It is never too late to be what you might have been."

DATE:

LOOKED FOR KEY SUPPORT &RESISTANCE LEVELS?	Y	N
ANALYSED YESTERDAY'S SESSION?	Y	N

		CHART ANALYSIS AND REASONS FOR ENTRY
TIME		
QUANTITY		
BUY PRICE		
SELL PRICE		
PROFIT (%)		
RISK REWARD		

WHAT I LEARNT FROM THIS TRADE		

WAS I IN THE CORRECT STATE OF MIND TO ENTER THIS TRADE?	Y	N
DID I USE POSITION SIZING PROPERLY?	Y	N
DID I FOLLOW ALL MY RULES?	Y	N
DID I REPEATE ANY OF MY OLD MISTAKES?	Y	N
AM I A BETTER TRADER THAN YESTERDAY?	Y	N

"When you change your thoughts, remember to also change your world."

REVIEW OF LAST 20 TRADES
Most successful strategy-
Worst performing strategy-
Best time for entry-
The Positives-
The Negatives-

DATE:

LOOKED FOR KEY SUPPORT &RESISTANCE LEVELS?	Y	N
ANALYSED YESTERDAY'S SESSION?	Y	N

		CHART ANALYSIS AND REASONS FOR ENTRY
TIME		
QUANTITY		
BUY PRICE		
SELL PRICE		
PROFIT (%)		
RISK REWARD		

WHAT I LEARNT FROM THIS TRADE		
WAS I IN THE CORRECT STATE OF MIND TO ENTER THIS TRADE?	Y	N
DID I USE POSITION SIZING PROPERLY?	Y	N
DID I FOLLOW ALL MY RULES?	Y	N
DID I REPEAT ANY OF MY OLD MISTAKES?	Y	N
AM I A BETTER TRADER THAN YESTERDAY?	Y	N

"A problem is a chance for you to do your best."

DATE:

LOOKED FOR KEY SUPPORT &RESISTANCE LEVELS?	Y	N
ANALYSED YESTERDAY'S SESSION?	Y	N

		CHART ANALYSIS AND REASONS FOR ENTRY
TIME		
QUANTITY		
BUY PRICE		
SELL PRICE		
PROFIT (%)		
RISK REWARD		

WHAT I LEARNT FROM THIS TRADE		

WAS I IN THE CORRECT STATE OF MIND TO ENTER THIS TRADE?	Y	N
DID I USE POSITION SIZING PROPERLY?	Y	N
DID I FOLLOW ALL MY RULES?	Y	N
DID I REPEAT ANY OF MY OLD MISTAKES?	Y	N
AM I A BETTER TRADER THAN YESTERDAY?	Y	N

"Love yourself first and everything else falls into line."

DATE:

LOOKED FOR KEY SUPPORT &RESISTANCE LEVELS?	Y	N
ANALYSED YESTERDAY'S SESSION?	Y	N

TIME	
QUANTITY	
BUY PRICE	
SELL PRICE	
PROFIT (%)	
RISK REWARD	

CHART ANALYSIS AND REASONS FOR ENTRY

WHAT I LEARNT FROM THIS TRADE

WAS I IN THE CORRECT STATE OF MIND TO ENTER THIS TRADE?	Y	N
DID I USE POSITION SIZING PROPERLY?	Y	N
DID I FOLLOW ALL MY RULES?	Y	N
DID I REPEAT ANY OF MY OLD MISTAKES?	Y	N
AM I A BETTER TRADER THAN YESTERDAY?	Y	N

"You will face many defeats in life, but never let yourself be defeated."

DATE:

LOOKED FOR KEY SUPPORT &RESISTANCE LEVELS?	Y	N
ANALYSED YESTERDAY'S SESSION?	Y	N

		CHART ANALYSIS AND REASONS FOR ENTRY
TIME		
QUANTITY		
BUY PRICE		
SELL PRICE		
PROFIT (%)		
RISK REWARD		

WHAT I LEARNT FROM THIS TRADE		
WAS I IN THE CORRECT STATE OF MIND TO ENTER THIS TRADE?	Y	N
DID I USE POSITION SIZING PROPERLY?	Y	N
DID I FOLLOW ALL MY RULES?	Y	N
DID I REPEAT ANY OF MY OLD MISTAKES?	Y	N
AM I A BETTER TRADER THAN YESTERDAY?	Y	N

"The question isn't who is going to let me; it's who is going to stop me."

DATE:

LOOKED FOR KEY SUPPORT &RESISTANCE LEVELS?	Y	N
ANALYSED YESTERDAY'S SESSION?	Y	N

TIME	
QUANTITY	
BUY PRICE	
SELL PRICE	
PROFIT (%)	
RISK REWARD	

CHART ANALYSIS AND REASONS FOR ENTRY

WHAT I LEARNT FROM THIS TRADE

WAS I IN THE CORRECT STATE OF MIND TO ENTER THIS TRADE?	Y	N
DID I USE POSITION SIZING PROPERLY?	Y	N
DID I FOLLOW ALL MY RULES?	Y	N
DID I REPEAT ANY OF MY OLD MISTAKES?	Y	N
AM I A BETTER TRADER THAN YESTERDAY?	Y	N

"Winning isn't everything, but wanting to win is."

DATE:

LOOKED FOR KEY SUPPORT &RESISTANCE LEVELS?	Y	N
ANALYSED YESTERDAY'S SESSION?	Y	N

		CHART ANALYSIS AND REASONS FOR ENTRY
TIME		
QUANTITY		
BUY PRICE		
SELL PRICE		
PROFIT (%)		
RISK REWARD		

WHAT I LEARNT FROM THIS TRADE		
WAS I IN THE CORRECT STATE OF MIND TO ENTER THIS TRADE?	Y	N
DID I USE POSITION SIZING PROPERLY?	Y	N
DID I FOLLOW ALL MY RULES?	Y	N
DID I REPEAT ANY OF MY OLD MISTAKES?	Y	N
AM I A BETTER TRADER THAN YESTERDAY?	Y	N

"Everything you've ever wanted is on the other side of fear."

DATE:

LOOKED FOR KEY SUPPORT &RESISTANCE LEVELS?	Y	N
ANALYSED YESTERDAY'S SESSION?	Y	N

		CHART ANALYSIS AND REASONS FOR ENTRY
TIME		
QUANTITY		
BUY PRICE		
SELL PRICE		
PROFIT (%)		
RISK REWARD		

WHAT I LEARNT FROM THIS TRADE		
WAS I IN THE CORRECT STATE OF MIND TO ENTER THIS TRADE?	Y	N
DID I USE POSITION SIZING PROPERLY?	Y	N
DID I FOLLOW ALL MY RULES?	Y	N
DID I REPEAT ANY OF MY OLD MISTAKES?	Y	N
AM I A BETTER TRADER THAN YESTERDAY?	Y	N

"Successful people do what unsuccessful people are not willing to do.
Don't wish it were easier; wish you were better."

DATE:

LOOKED FOR KEY SUPPORT &RESISTANCE LEVELS?	Y	N
ANALYSED YESTERDAY'S SESSION?	Y	N

		CHART ANALYSIS AND REASONS FOR ENTRY
TIME		
QUANTITY		
BUY PRICE		
SELL PRICE		
PROFIT (%)		
RISK REWARD		

WHAT I LEARNT FROM THIS TRADE		
WAS I IN THE CORRECT STATE OF MIND TO ENTER THIS TRADE?	Y	N
DID I USE POSITION SIZING PROPERLY?	Y	N
DID I FOLLOW ALL MY RULES?	Y	N
DID I REPEAT ANY OF MY OLD MISTAKES?	Y	N
AM I A BETTER TRADER THAN YESTERDAY?	Y	N

"A successful man is one who can lay a firm foundation with the bricks others have thrown at him."

DATE:

LOOKED FOR KEY SUPPORT &RESISTANCE LEVELS?	Y	N
ANALYSED YESTERDAY'S SESSION?	Y	N

		CHART ANALYSIS AND REASONS FOR ENTRY
TIME		
QUANTITY		
BUY PRICE		
SELL PRICE		
PROFIT (%)		
RISK REWARD		

WHAT I LEARNT FROM THIS TRADE		
WAS I IN THE CORRECT STATE OF MIND TO ENTER THIS TRADE?	Y	N
DID I USE POSITION SIZING PROPERLY?	Y	N
DID I FOLLOW ALL MY RULES?	Y	N
DID I REPEAT ANY OF MY OLD MISTAKES?	Y	N
AM I A BETTER TRADER THAN YESTERDAY?	Y	N

"Success is a matter of sticking to a set of common-sense principles anyone can master."

DATE:

LOOKED FOR KEY SUPPORT &RESISTANCE LEVELS?	Y	N
ANALYSED YESTERDAY'S SESSION?	Y	N

		CHART ANALYSIS AND REASONS FOR ENTRY
TIME		
QUANTITY		
BUY PRICE		
SELL PRICE		
PROFIT (%)		
RISK REWARD		

WHAT I LEARNT FROM THIS TRADE		
WAS I IN THE CORRECT STATE OF MIND TO ENTER THIS TRADE?	Y	N
DID I USE POSITION SIZING PROPERLY?	Y	N
DID I FOLLOW ALL MY RULES?	Y	N
DID I REPEAT ANY OF MY OLD MISTAKES?	Y	N
AM I A BETTER TRADER THAN YESTERDAY?	Y	N

"It's fun to do the impossible."

DATE:

LOOKED FOR KEY SUPPORT &RESISTANCE LEVELS?	Y	N
ANALYSED YESTERDAY'S SESSION?	Y	N

		CHART ANALYSIS AND REASONS FOR ENTRY
TIME		
QUANTITY		
BUY PRICE		
SELL PRICE		
PROFIT (%)		
RISK REWARD		

WHAT I LEARNT FROM THIS TRADE		
WAS I IN THE CORRECT STATE OF MIND TO ENTER THIS TRADE?	Y	N
DID I USE POSITION SIZING PROPERLY?	Y	N
DID I FOLLOW ALL MY RULES?	Y	N
DID I REPEAT ANY OF MY OLD MISTAKES?	Y	N
AM I A BETTER TRADER THAN YESTERDAY?	Y	N

"No one would have crossed the ocean if he could have gotten off the ship in the storm."

DATE:

LOOKED FOR KEY SUPPORT &RESISTANCE LEVELS?	Y	N
ANALYSED YESTERDAY'S SESSION?	Y	N

		CHART ANALYSIS AND REASONS FOR ENTRY
TIME		
QUANTITY		
BUY PRICE		
SELL PRICE		
PROFIT (%)		
RISK REWARD		

WHAT I LEARNT FROM THIS TRADE		
WAS I IN THE CORRECT STATE OF MIND TO ENTER THIS TRADE?	Y	N
DID I USE POSITION SIZING PROPERLY?	Y	N
DID I FOLLOW ALL MY RULES?	Y	N
DID I REPEAT ANY OF MY OLD MISTAKES?	Y	N
AM I A BETTER TRADER THAN YESTERDAY?	Y	N

"Hard work beats talent when talent doesn't work hard."

DATE:

LOOKED FOR KEY SUPPORT &RESISTANCE LEVELS?	Y	N
ANALYSED YESTERDAY'S SESSION?	Y	N

		CHART ANALYSIS AND REASONS FOR ENTRY
TIME		
QUANTITY		
BUY PRICE		
SELL PRICE		
PROFIT (%)		
RISK REWARD		

WHAT I LEARNT FROM THIS TRADE		
WAS I IN THE CORRECT STATE OF MIND TO ENTER THIS TRADE?	Y	N
DID I USE POSITION SIZING PROPERLY?	Y	N
DID I FOLLOW ALL MY RULES?	Y	N
DID I REPEAT ANY OF MY OLD MISTAKES?	Y	N
AM I A BETTER TRADER THAN YESTERDAY?	Y	N

"Don't spend time beating on a wall, hoping to transform it into a door."

DATE:

LOOKED FOR KEY SUPPORT &RESISTANCE LEVELS?	Y	N
ANALYSED YESTERDAY'S SESSION?	Y	N

TIME	
QUANTITY	
BUY PRICE	
SELL PRICE	
PROFIT (%)	
RISK REWARD	

CHART ANALYSIS AND REASONS FOR ENTRY

WHAT I LEARNT FROM THIS TRADE

WAS I IN THE CORRECT STATE OF MIND TO ENTER THIS TRADE?	Y	N
DID I USE POSITION SIZING PROPERLY?	Y	N
DID I FOLLOW ALL MY RULES?	Y	N
DID I REPEAT ANY OF MY OLD MISTAKES?	Y	N
AM I A BETTER TRADER THAN YESTERDAY?	Y	N

"It is our attitude at the beginning of a difficult task which, more than anything else, will affect its successful outcome."

DATE:

LOOKED FOR KEY SUPPORT &RESISTANCE LEVELS?	Y	N
ANALYSED YESTERDAY'S SESSION?	Y	N

		CHART ANALYSIS AND REASONS FOR ENTRY
TIME		
QUANTITY		
BUY PRICE		
SELL PRICE		
PROFIT (%)		
RISK REWARD		

WHAT I LEARNT FROM THIS TRADE		

WAS I IN THE CORRECT STATE OF MIND TO ENTER THIS TRADE?	Y	N
DID I USE POSITION SIZING PROPERLY?	Y	N
DID I FOLLOW ALL MY RULES?	Y	N
DID I REPEAT ANY OF MY OLD MISTAKES?	Y	N
AM I A BETTER TRADER THAN YESTERDAY?	Y	N

"Success depends upon previous preparation, and without such preparation, there is sure to be failure."

DATE:

LOOKED FOR KEY SUPPORT &RESISTANCE LEVELS?	Y	N
ANALYSED YESTERDAY'S SESSION?	Y	N

TIME	
QUANTITY	
BUY PRICE	
SELL PRICE	
PROFIT (%)	
RISK REWARD	

CHART ANALYSIS AND REASONS FOR ENTRY

WHAT I LEARNT FROM THIS TRADE		
WAS I IN THE CORRECT STATE OF MIND TO ENTER THIS TRADE?	Y	N
DID I USE POSITION SIZING PROPERLY?	Y	N
DID I FOLLOW ALL MY RULES?	Y	N
DID I REPEAT ANY OF MY OLD MISTAKES?	Y	N
AM I A BETTER TRADER THAN YESTERDAY?	Y	N

"The pain you feel today is the strength you feel tomorrow. For every challenge encountered, there is opportunity for growth

DATE:

LOOKED FOR KEY SUPPORT &RESISTANCE LEVELS?	Y	N
ANALYSED YESTERDAY'S SESSION?	Y	N

TIME	
QUANTITY	
BUY PRICE	
SELL PRICE	
PROFIT (%)	
RISK REWARD	

CHART ANALYSIS AND REASONS FOR ENTRY

WHAT I LEARNT FROM THIS TRADE

WAS I IN THE CORRECT STATE OF MIND TO ENTER THIS TRADE?	Y	N
DID I USE POSITION SIZING PROPERLY?	Y	N
DID I FOLLOW ALL MY RULES?	Y	N
DID I REPEAT ANY OF MY OLD MISTAKES?	Y	N
AM I A BETTER TRADER THAN YESTERDAY?	Y	N

"Every day you spend at work is a foundation for your future."

DATE:

LOOKED FOR KEY SUPPORT &RESISTANCE LEVELS?	Y	N
ANALYSED YESTERDAY'S SESSION?	Y	N

		CHART ANALYSIS AND REASONS FOR ENTRY
TIME		
QUANTITY		
BUY PRICE		
SELL PRICE		
PROFIT (%)		
RISK REWARD		

WHAT I LEARNT FROM THIS TRADE		
WAS I IN THE CORRECT STATE OF MIND TO ENTER THIS TRADE?	Y	N
DID I USE POSITION SIZING PROPERLY?	Y	N
DID I FOLLOW ALL MY RULES?	Y	N
DID I REPEAT ANY OF MY OLD MISTAKES?	Y	N
AM I A BETTER TRADER THAN YESTERDAY?	Y	N

"I am not a product of my circumstances. I am a product of my decisions."

DATE:

LOOKED FOR KEY SUPPORT &RESISTANCE LEVELS?	Y	N
ANALYSED YESTERDAY'S SESSION?	Y	N

TIME	
QUANTITY	
BUY PRICE	
SELL PRICE	
PROFIT (%)	
RISK REWARD	

CHART ANALYSIS AND REASONS FOR ENTRY

WHAT I LEARNT FROM THIS TRADE

WAS I IN THE CORRECT STATE OF MIND TO ENTER THIS TRADE?	Y	N
DID I USE POSITION SIZING PROPERLY?	Y	N
DID I FOLLOW ALL MY RULES?	Y	N
DID I REPEAT ANY OF MY OLD MISTAKES?	Y	N
AM I A BETTER TRADER THAN YESTERDAY?	Y	N

"We cannot solve problems with the kind of thinking we employed when we came up with them."

DATE:

LOOKED FOR KEY SUPPORT &RESISTANCE LEVELS?	Y	N
ANALYSED YESTERDAY'S SESSION?	Y	N

		CHART ANALYSIS AND REASONS FOR ENTRY
TIME		
QUANTITY		
BUY PRICE		
SELL PRICE		
PROFIT (%)		
RISK REWARD		

WHAT I LEARNT FROM THIS TRADE		

WAS I IN THE CORRECT STATE OF MIND TO ENTER THIS TRADE?	Y	N
DID I USE POSITION SIZING PROPERLY?	Y	N
DID I FOLLOW ALL MY RULES?	Y	N
DID I REPEAT ANY OF MY OLD MISTAKES?	Y	N
AM I A BETTER TRADER THAN YESTERDAY?	Y	N

"Success is stumbling from failure to failure with no loss of enthusiasm."

DATE:

REVIEW OF LAST 20 TRADES

Most successful strategy-

Worst performing strategy-

Best time for entry-

The Positives-

The Negatives-

www.ingramcontent.com/pod-product-compliance
Lightning Source LLC
Chambersburg PA
CBHW040741150726
48196CB00061B/1483